The Choices
We Make

Dictate The Life We Lead

The Choices We Make

Dictate The Life We Lead

105 Lessons To Help You Make The Right Choices

By Eric M. Daniels

authorHOUSE®

AuthorHouse™
1663 Liberty Drive
Bloomington, IN 47403
www.authorhouse.com
Phone: 1-800-839-8640

Published by AuthorHouse   10/12/2012

ISBN: 978-1-4772-7107-0 (sc)
ISBN: 978-1-4772-7108-7 (hc)
ISBN: 978-1-4772-7109-4 (e)

Library of Congress Control Number: 2012917145

Thanks to Donna Puglisi for her editing, and Michele Haro for the cover photograph.

Thanks also to my friends Karen Skurla and Tom Desmond for their advice and guidance.

A very special thanks to my wife, Denise Verderosa Daniels, for her love, patience and encouragement.

This one is for Jonathan, whose story has yet to be told.

AUTHOR'S NOTE

There are two sides to every story. The recollections told in this book are my side and my side only. To protect those unable to tell their side, some names have been changed and others have been omitted.

Eric Daniels

PROLOGUE

I've made many choices in my life, a good deal, of which have been bad ones. When I was real young, I made typical moronic choices that any kid would make. As I grew older, I didn't necessarily grow smarter, because I was still making poor choices in many areas of my life. Now, more than half my life is over and it seems I'm still doing the same old things.

We read books all the time telling us how to live a good life. We read quotes from famous and successful people. We can even attend a plethora of seminars on making the right choices and becoming successful at whatever it is we want to do.

To date, I have never read a real life story with real people, real experiences, and real lessons built right in. So, I decided to write this autobiography. It doesn't have all the answers to life, but it's real, and its lessons are pertinent to everyday living.

Some of these lessons I have learned and some I am still learning. I don't claim to be a wise sage, just a guy who knows what it's like to screw up, and I'm a bit smarter for having done so. However, if I knew then what I know now, I would have taken a completely different path in life.

We will all be faced with many choices in our lifetime. Wouldn't it be nice to make the right choice every time? Whatever choices you make, just remember, "The Choices We Make Dictate The Life We Lead".

A Word About The Title
And The Lessons

The idea for the title of this book came from the movie "Renaissance Man". Danny DeVito, playing a teacher for army basic training recruits who needed extra help in the academic area, taught them many things. One of the things he said to the students was, "The choices you make dictate the life you lead". He followed that with, "To thine own self be true".

You will notice both of these as lessons in this book and you will notice the title as a lesson many times over. Any lesson I ever learned always drew me back to my choices.

Some of the "Lessons" are quotes or sayings that, no doubt, you have heard before. Not knowing where some of these quotes originated, I cannot give proper credit to them, only to say that I did not come up with them myself. They are a compilation of things I've heard or read over my lifetime from different sources. I'd like to thank the brilliant minds that have coined these phrases, and at the same time apologize for not knowing who they all are. Some of the lessons are original, however, and I can only hope that they all will help you in making the right choices.

CONTENTS

INTRODUCTION

The U.S. Navy had a commercial out a few years ago where their motto was "U.S. Navy, it's not just a job, it's an adventure". At the beginning of the commercial, the announcer asks, "If someone wrote a book about your life, would anybody want to read it?" The premise, of course, is that the navy would offer you an exciting and interesting life.

Being an army veteran, I had my doubts about the so-called "adventure" the navy offered, but the question about the book really made me think. I'm not one to think of myself as anything special, so I never pursued the idea.

My friend, Janis Taylor, is a computer expert who started a blog on the web. I found it interesting when I read her stories, but I thought, "She's my friend, of course I find it interesting." Would I have enjoyed her blog had I not known her? I wasn't sure.

Janis kept telling me that I should create my own blog website because everything she knew about me and saw me do was intriguing to her. She said a lot of people would enjoy reading my stories, whether they knew me or not.

Well, all I've been through has taught me a lot. Wisdom truly does come with experience and age. If my life story is interesting to anyone, so be it. It's filled with happiness, sadness, good times, bad times, fun times, trying times, mistakes, victory, defeat, honor, dishonor, love, hate, intrigue, and of course, more mistakes. Through it all, I have gained wisdom. If nothing else, I hope this book shows my children, grandchildren, and great grandchildren what I've been through, how I survived, and why I am who I am. Perhaps a small amount of what I share will stay with them, and help mold each of them into the beautiful person I always wanted myself to be.

This is the head start I never had. And for everyone else, may you laugh, cry, and relate to my personal experiences. I hope you may also gain some wisdom.

Eric M. Daniels

CHAPTER 1

From The Beginning

I was the second born to Ray and Phoebe Daniels on November 7, 1962 at JB Thomas Hospital in Peabody, Mass. My sister, Maria (Mini), was 11 months older than me. After that came Maureen (Mo), Raymond Jr. (Sudsy), Anthony (Rusty), and Deidre (Dee).

My parents married in 1960, which was a year after my father graduated from high school, and the year my mother was supposed to graduate. She never graduated, and the shit's been hitting the fan ever since.

Too young, and mistakenly in love, these two intelligent, good looking people with the best of intentions, began twenty years of what I can only describe as "Hell".

Not all my childhood was terrible. My mom's parents, Grammy and Grampy lived next door, which was always a safe refuge whenever I needed to escape.

The other wonderful thing about my childhood was the neighborhood. It was full of kids all the time. Never was there a moment that I couldn't find someone to play with. We played with trucks, we sang, we played sports, we laughed, and we even fought. But oh, what a neighborhood to grow up in! I didn't know it then, but all the kids were my "real" family.

Going to school was a real drag for me, and I always thought I was stupid, but I'll talk more on this later. Suffice it to say, my stomach was in knots at home, and again, every day at school. That doesn't leave much time to enjoy life. Somehow, because of the neighborhood kids, I did manage to enjoy all my time away from home and school.

As soon as I turned 18, I hightailed it out of there faster than a speeding bullet. With a pregnant 17-year-old girlfriend (and later wife), I had to become a man quickly. As difficult as it was, it was far easier being in control of my own life and bringing up a family than it ever was growing up as Ray and Phoebe's kid and Maria's little brother.

Three kids, ten years in the army and 16 years of marriage to the only woman I ever knew and loved, brought me to a new phase in life. I had a new occupation, new state to live in, new wife, and two new children as well. Add a few more years, and two more kids, and you have a very busy and crazy life.

Eight years later after relocating again and hoping to settle down comfortably with just my wife, out comes that guy with the club who's been waiting around the corner. Strike two with the marriage thing came when my second wife didn't feel secure enough to move down to Florida from New Hampshire after I had been there almost two years alone. I made the grave mistake of thinking her unconditional love for me would outweigh my own selfish ambitions. Yet another failure in my life, but one I've gained more wisdom from than any other circumstance I have ever been in.

LESSON 1—UNCONDITIONAL LOVE DESERVES TO BE RECIPROCATED.

My life has been one learning experience after another. I never did well in school, and they taught me the lesson before I took the test. In real life, you take the test first and then you learn your lesson. It's not easy, but whose life is? It's how we handle life's little battles that we become a better person with each day.

CHAPTER 2

Relative Annoyance

Relatives can be both a blessing and an annoyance. One particular relative of mine, who shall remain nameless, was more on the annoying side for me. My parents thought this relative could do no wrong. To be fair, this person did help my dad out a lot when my mom was in the funny farm. It seemed every year my parents would have this huge fight, and off to the mental hospital my mother went for a few months. Because they helped dad out a great deal, he overlooked anything this person did wrong.

My brother Ray and I were on the receiving end of an ass whipping solely due to this relative more than any other thing in our lives. If you don't remember anything else in this book, remember this,

LESSON 2—KARMA NEVER FORGETS.

I remember going fishing with my best friend Steve Chigas (who we all called, Farn—short for Stefano), and his grandpa, Pooley. What a great day!

We got in this little rowboat, and anchored about 50 feet from the shore. The moment our lines hit the water, all three of us got a bite at the same time. We hit a whole school of flounder. That was my first time fishing, and boy was I happy! We couldn't put the bait on the hooks fast enough. It was exhilarating being 15 years old, out on a boat with my best friend, catching one fish after another. Two hours later they were still biting, and we had so many fish that we had to stop because we ran out of room in the boat. We took home well over a hundred that day.

Back at Farn's house, we cleaned and gutted every one of them while trying to dodge the yellow jacket wasps they attracted. When we were done, I had a big pile of beautiful flounder to take home to feed my family for dinner that night.

When I got home I set the table, mixed the batter, got out the pans, and was ready to rock and roll. I was so proud of catching all those fish and even more excited to be able to cook them for my whole family.

It didn't quite work out the way I would have liked. You see, that annoying relative thing reared its ugly head when they insisted I leave the kitchen to them. When I refused, a call went out to my dad who came swiftly along to let me know in no uncertain terms that I wouldn't be doing the cooking that night. That lesson came with a little physical reminder just to make sure I got the message.

I recall a time when I was wearing my own pair of jeans that I was accused of steeling from the annoying one. Another shout out to good ole dad found those jeans abruptly pulled off my waist along with anything else I was wearing. The most embarrassing part of the entire episode was that it was done in view of my other family members.

I can't even begin to express my embarrassment at that age. Everyone was too scared to even move so they all just stared at me while my father handed the pants to my accuser. After he left the room, I ran upstairs in disbelief. To this day, I can't stand to be naked, not in front of my wife, not even alone.

LESSON 3—PARENTS NEED TO THINK BEFORE EVERY ACTION THEY TAKE TOWARDS THEIR CHILDREN. ONE MISTAKE OUT OF ANGER COULD SCAR YOUR CHILD FOR A LIFETIME.

It wasn't that this relative was a bad person. They were spoiled and encouraged to be that way towards all of us. In fact, the pressure this person was put under from a very young age was immense.

LESSON 4—CHILDREN SHOULD BE CHILDREN. NEVER SHOULD ANY CHILD BE GIVEN THE RESPONSIBILITY OF AN ADULT. IT ROBS THEM OF THEIR CHILDHOOD, AND GIVES THEM A FALSE SENSE OF SECURITY.

All in all, they did a good job helping my parents, but at a price too high to handle. They unknowingly alienated themselves from everyone around them.

I wish no ill will on anyone, but we should all know that what goes around comes around. Things are miserable some days for this relative and I can't help but think maybe, just maybe if they were a bit nicer in days gone by, that perhaps life would not have been so cruel.

LESSON 5—WE ALL PAY IN SOME WAY FOR OUR MISTAKES, EVEN IF WE ARE FORGIVEN.

Even with all that's been said, we will all be there for anyone in our family no matter what has happened in the past. We learned a long time ago that:

LESSON 6—WHEN ALL IS SAID AND DONE, THE ONLY THING YOU HAVE LEFT IS YOUR FAMILY.

CHAPTER 3

Dad

I owe a lot to my father. He showed me what it takes to support a large family. He instilled in me the drive and determination to be the best. He imparted so many words of wisdom I still refer to and live by to this very day. He taught me how to work hard and showed me the value in being honest to everyone. I learned from him how important it is to read and to always expand my horizons. I was constantly reminded of the virtues of decency, selflessness, goodwill, altruism, and kindness towards others. Of course, the best advice he ever gave me was:

LESSON 7—BE A GIVER, NOT A TAKER.

Sound advice wasn't the only way my dad taught me. My brother and I got a gift of a set of boxing gloves one holiday and we thought that was the greatest gift ever. Then one day they ended up on the kitchen table as a reminder that we did something wrong. We knew then that it was time to learn how to box, old school in the kitchen with Dad. It was painful at times and I can't say that I didn't learn how to protect myself, but I probably would have rather had karate lessons or something a bit more organized.

LESSON 8—HAVE YOUR CHILDREN LEARN SELF DEFENSE, BUT LET A PROFESSIONAL TEACH IT.

To this day, I love physical competition, as long as I am in the middle of it, either giving or getting a beating. I think I enjoy it today because I'm bigger and stronger as an adult, and I constantly challenge myself to take on all comers. Win, lose or draw, I love a good fight.

Dad tried to teach us responsibility. I remember the day he gave us the task of digging up twelve poles around our yard. My brother and I had all day to do it. I started at 8 AM digging and digging and digging. My brother decided to put it off and go hang out with his friends. Consequently, only seven poles were dug up. When my dad got home and saw the job was not done, he promptly made us quit the Pop Warner football team we both played for.

I wouldn't have minded if I could have played the following year, but this was my last year of eligibility before junior high, and I was so excited because at the end of the season I was getting a jacket and a trophy, something tangible that I could look at every day and be reminded of actually accomplishing something. It really didn't matter to my younger brother, who had two years left to play. I never understood why I got that harsh punishment even though I did my share.

LESSON 9—DOLE OUT PUNISHMENT AND DISCIPLINE FAIRLY. UNLESS YOU ARE IN THE MILITARY, YOU SHOULD NEVER PUNISH A GROUP FOR THE ACTIONS OF ONE.

Believe me, I did enough on my own to get in hot water with my dad. I didn't need Ray's help, when I was in eleventh grade and I came home with a second quarter report card with straight F's. I never was a bright student. God knows, I really didn't try very hard at my academics. I missed half the quarter after knee surgery. The tutor never submitted my grades. So when I brought the report card home, I begged my mother not to show my father. She promised me she wouldn't tell him, but she showed him the report card as soon as he came home.

LESSON 10—IF YOU MAKE A PROMISE, YOU BETTER KEEP IT. YOUR ENTIRE CHARACTER DEPENDS ON YOUR WORD.

Suffice it to say that day was not the best day of my life. I can't even begin to explain the uncomfortable and hurtful feelings both physically and mentally that I endured for a relatively minor infraction. I didn't see the pressures my father was under, not that I deserved everything he did to me, although I did earn some of it.

I asked my dad one day when he was in a good mood, "Dad, why are you always in a bad mood when you wake up?" He answered, "If you had to face the days I face, you'd be in a bad mood too". Once I got older I understood exactly what he meant. However, I wasn't older, I was just a kid.

LESSON 11—NEVER EXPECT A CHILD TO UNDERSTAND AN ADULT'S WORLD. THEY WILL HAVE PLENTY OF TIME FOR THAT WHEN THEY ARE ADULTS.

My father worked extremely hard as the Housing Authority Director of a large city, a job he secured at age 28, which, back then, was unheard of. He truly was a genius, and he did so many good things for so many people. Upon his retirement, the last city he worked for erected a building in his name. I wasn't surprised to find out that my father never showed up for the dedication ceremony, because he didn't ask for or want the recognition. He was a doer. He never cared about who got the credit, just about getting the job done.

LESSON 12—IT DOESN'T MATTER WHERE THE CREDIT GOES. WORRY ABOUT GETTING THE JOB DONE AND THE CREDIT WILL TAKE CARE OF ITSELF.

Between work and trying to keep the wolves from the door, he never had much time for me or any of my siblings. I wanted to spend time with him when he wasn't angry and wasn't busy with something. He never had the time. He never said, "Good morning," "Happy Birthday", "Merry Christmas" or "I love you". It's no wonder I have difficulties with close relationships. I have a natural instinct to love and care, but I have a difficult time expressing that love. I'm always putting up a wall when I get overwhelmed. I was told that putting up the wall when I was a child was a way for me to handle all of the pain. As an adult, I no longer need to put up the wall. It was a good way to cope when I was a kid, but it's the wrong way to cope as an adult.

LESSON 13—BREAK DOWN THE WALLS OF RESISTANCE AND FACE EACH PROBLEM IN LIFE HEAD ON. DENIAL DOES NOT MAKE YOUR PROBLEMS GO AWAY.

All in all, I learned a lot from my father, what I should do and what I shouldn't. As time went on, he became a different man. He became calm, kind, funny and still filled with great stories of wisdom. He also went through the death of a son, his wife's diagnosis with esophageal cancer, and then his own diagnosis with colon cancer.

Since my brother died in 1992 at the age of 27, my father hadn't been the same. Like any parent who lost a child, he suffered daily. He would go to the cemetery every single day for years after Sudsy died, just to sit there by the grave and water the grass. He would bring his own chair and hose, and just sit. You couldn't find a prettier gravesite in the entire cemetery. The grass was like a golf green, and he changed the flowers monthly.

LESSON 14—DO FOR AND LOVE PEOPLE WHILE THEY ARE ALIVE. WATERING THE GRASS OF YOUR RELATIONSHIP IS MUCH LESS PAINFUL THAN WATERING THE GRASS OF A GRAVE.

He consequently went through a very painful bout with colon cancer that spread to his liver. He endured operations, chemotherapy, hours of doctor visits, and a heart attack in the same period. Then he waited to die. He was in horrific pain up to the very last minute. I can't help but think that it didn't have to be like that.

LESSON 15—LIFE'S NOT FAIR.

CHAPTER 4

Mary Anne

My adolescence would have been nothing but pure misery if it hadn't been for my first wife and best friend since sixth grade, Mary Anne. Sure, I had my grandparents living next door, and they did make a difference, but there's something about a non-family member from the opposite sex giving you attention and love that changes everything.

Today, Mary Anne and I are friends, but we'd both tell you that we were simply not compatible. Well, we were when we were kids, but with age, we grew apart. Still, as a kid with issues such as I had, Mare (as I called her then) was my saving grace.

The very first day I met her I was smitten. I was 12, and the neighborhood kids were playing football on a local vacant lot we all called "The Field". The boys and girls all played together no matter what the sport was. My friends from Forest Street brought their cousin from out of town to play along. One look at her and I just melted.

I remember making a wisecrack about her height because she was so short. It was my way of getting her attention by acting cool. I probably started off on the wrong foot because, as I recall, she retorted with a nasty comment about my acne. I believe she called me "Raw hamburger face". Looking back, I obviously deserved what I got, and believe me, I was quite embarrassed.

LESSON 16—IF YOU WANT SOMEONE'S ATTENTION AND AFFECTION, BEING SWEET BEATS BEING COOL EVERYTIME.

We got over our first meeting, and somehow she seemed to like me. I would only see her periodically at her cousin's house, and I naturally wanted to impress her. I remember one day my brother Ray purchased a pair of sneakers for me from Thom McCann Shoe store for ninety-nine cents. He was so happy that he found such a good deal. These were the ugliest sneakers you ever saw, but I wore them around the neighborhood so my brother wouldn't be offended.

I went to Mare's cousin's house to see her this one time, and boy did she look pretty. As I was showing off to her, she kept looking down at my shoes, then looking at me with this weird face as if to say, "What the hell is your problem?" I just knew she was about to bust on my new sneakers. At that point, I had to make a decision. Leave the ugly sneakers on and spare my brother's feelings, or go home and change in order to salvage some of my dignity with this girl. Well, my dignity outweighed my feelings for my brother this time. After changing back into my regular sneakers, I went back to see Mare with all the confidence in the world. It wasn't until after we were married that I mentioned this incident to her, and she told me that she remembered it as well, but it wasn't the sneakers she thought were weird, it was my "flood" pants! So I went the entire time thinking everything was great after getting those ugly sneakers out of my life without knowing it was my pants that turned her off!

LESSON 17—WHAT YOU DON'T KNOW CAN'T HURT YOU.

Hey, she still married me, right?

I knew she cared about me because whenever I called her with all my troubles, she would cry right along with me. She hated to see me sad, and it made her sad.

LESSON 18—DEEP DOWN EMPATHY FOR ANOTHER'S PLIGHT IS A MEASURE OF LOVE THAT THE OTHER PERSON WILL NEVER FORGET.

When I was 16, I got a job working in a local tannery. I grew up in Peabody, Mass., and we were known as the "leather capitol of the U.S." In fact, our high school team is called the "Peabody Tanners". (In fairness to Woburn, Mass., they are also called the "Tanners" for the same reason). At any rate, working in a leather factory was hard work. I worked with Greek and Portuguese people who barely spoke English. I did everything from pulling skins from the wet wheels to trimming, buffing, shaving, dry milling, pasting, tacking, and I even worked in the shipping room. It was decent money, but the hardest work I've ever done. It was miserable in the summer, hot and steamy, like a sauna. I couldn't wait to take a shower at the end of the day to brush off all the cockroaches that got under my clothes.

I remember one particular day in the summer Mare came to bring me lunch. She had a jacket dry cleaned for me on a hanger and a brown bag with two tuna sandwiches, potato chips and homemade brownies. It felt so good to have someone care about me enough to do such a nice thing. There were a lot of other fun things she could have been doing on that beautiful summer day, but she choose to take the time to prepare my lunch, bake brownies, and walk two miles in the blazing sun to bring it to me. I realized then that I was important to her. So now, I always try to go out of my way to show people that are important to me how much I love them.

LESSON 19—KINDNESS IS MAGNIFIED WHEN YOU GO OUT OF YOUR WAY TO HELP OTHERS, ESPECIALLY WHEN YOU ARE INCONVENIENCED. ANYONE CAN BE NICE WHEN IT'S EASY, BUT NOT EVERYONE CAN BE NICE WHEN IT'S HARD.

I was so in love with her that I truly was happy when I learned she was pregnant. The problems, however, were many. She was 16 years old, in eleventh grade, with a mother who hated me, and a father who had died the year before. I was in twelfth grade, failing miserably, with no home life to speak of and no idea what lay ahead of me.

After a meeting with her mom, I was told she was going away. One month later, Mare, her two brothers and her mother, drove a U-Haul to Florida.

It would be 5 months before I would see her again. She got off the plane in Boston a little heavier than when I last saw her, but still as beautiful as ever. The powers that be finally relented after months of prodding by other family members. After listening to Mare cry every day, they reluctantly let Mare come back to Boston to be with me, without their blessing of course.

Thank God for her Aunt Pat and her Uncle Jerry. They became our second parents through our entire relationship. The support and love they showed towards me was astounding. I would later in life, by virtue of my divorce with Mare, ruin my relationship with them. To this day it is one of my deepest regrets.

Mare and I got married on Valentines Day in 1981. On March 30, 1981, our daughter Jessica was born. So now she was a high school dropout. I had just completed summer school in August so I could get my diploma. We started our new life.

We had no vehicle, no money, no education and nowhere to go but up.

LESSON 20—WHEN THINGS ARE REALLY BAD, YOU HAVE TO KNOW THAT IT CAN ONLY GET BETTER, BECAUSE IT WILL.

I had four jobs while Mare stayed home with the baby. From 6am to 3pm I worked at the leather factory Monday through Friday. On Tuesdays and Thursdays I worked as a security guard from 4pm to 10pm. On Wednesdays, Fridays and Saturdays I did dishes and later cooked at a seafood restaurant. On Sundays 9am-5pm I made ice cream at my uncle's business, Richardson's Dairy in Middleton, Mass. Mare also did some daycare at the house a few days a week. We did all this with no vehicle.

I try to explain this to young people today but they don't believe me. Kids today are given so much that they have an attitude of entitlement. Sometimes I think my generation failed in many areas concerning our children. We gave them all the things we didn't have because we wanted to be good parents and it backfired on us. I'm not saying all the kids are bad, I just think we (my generation) screwed up.

LESSON 21—NO ONE OWES YOU A DAMN THING. WORK FOR WHAT YOU GET, AND YOU WILL GET WHAT YOU EARN.

We did get some help along the way. After all, no man is an island. Mare's grandfather gave us an old Ford Maverick after he could no longer drive. My grandfather would let us borrow his car before that, so we weren't totally without transportation all the time. On the other hand, I walked to all of my jobs except the one on Sunday at the dairy.

I had always wanted to be a funeral director, but I had no education and no idea how to get into the business. I remember going to all of the funeral homes in my area and trying to get any information I could about what it would take to get my foot in the door. Every funeral director I spoke with told me the same thing. No education, no family in the business and no money . . . give it up. I remember taking pictures of all the funeral homes on the North Shore of Boston, and dreaming that one-day I too, would have my very own. I even went to the embalming school in Boston, and purchased a book called "The Principles and Practice of Embalming". It was the text of the day for embalming students all over the country. I read it every day for years before I entered embalming school twelve years later.

All the work I was putting in with nothing to show for it other than survival, made me think. I can't do this for the rest of my life. So I found out that the army had a Military Occupational Specialty (MOS) called Graves Registration. I thought I could join the army as a Graves

Registration Specialist and it would be a step in the right direction towards my goal of becoming a real mortician.

I must say that at this point in my life I had already taken the ASVAB (Armed Services Vocational Aptitude Battery Test), trying to get into the air force and I failed. I didn't even score high enough to qualify for entrance to the air force! Two years earlier, I took my SAT's and scored better than only 10% of the country. Basically, I was a dummy. I went to the army recruiter without consulting my wife. The recruiter told me there were no openings for Graves Registration but that I could sign up for paratrooper duty and always transfer once I got in. I went home that day and told Mary Anne that I joined the army. Not exactly the best way to go about things, but it did work out. My wife was supportive of me.

LESSON 22—DON'T BE AFRAID TO GO FOR YOUR DREAMS, BUT NEVER MAKE ANY MAJOR DECISION WITHOUT CONSULTING YOUR SPOUSE.

Ten years of the army brought us two more children. Stefanie was born at Ft. Bragg, NC, in 1984, and Joey was born in Balboa, Panama, in 1986. Mary Anne and I struggled financially and also with our relationship for quite a while. We fought all the time when I was stationed at Ft. Bragg. When she was pregnant with Stefanie, we got into an argument and she dug her fingernails in my face. She scratched the top of my forehead down to my chin. I went to work the next day with nasty scratch marks all over my face. You can imagine my embarrassment when I was asked about what happened. I don't remember what I did, but I'm sure I deserved it.

I re-enlisted for another three-year tour, this time in Panama. I went to Panama first because Mary Anne was unsure if she wanted to join me. She reluctantly came after I was there for four months. I was on thin ice with her, so I was on my best behavior.

I was thrilled when she arrived with Jessica and Stefanie in January of 1986. It was more of the same for us, getting along one week, and hating each other the next. Despite this, she was very supportive of my career and became a leader in the family support group.

I went off to Honduras for a four month TDY tour while my family stayed behind in Panama. While there, I met a very nice girl, about my age, named Jessica. Her father was a farmer in Tegucigalpa (The Honduras Capital). I was very intrigued with the way they lived, and I enjoyed learning first-hand about another culture. I wasn't doing anything wrong, so I shared my experiences and stories openly with my wife. She wasn't too keen on that, so I backed off with my stories for a while.

About a year after I returned from Honduras, I tried to call my friend Jessica in the presence of my wife. I wanted to say hello and see how she and her family were doing. In my mind I had a friend from another part of the world and I thought it was great. Well, Mary Anne didn't quite see it that way. In fact, to this day, she maintains that I cheated on her with this girl from Honduras. It never happened, but I learned that sometimes you can share too much, causing people to wonder what you've been up to.

LESSON 23—SOME THINGS ARE BETTER LEFT UNSAID.

We rode out the storm for the rest of my tour in Panama, and then it was off to my favorite place in the whole world . . . . Hawaii. I can easily say that the four years we spent in Hawaii were the best years of our life as a family. At the same time, however, I could feel my bond with Mary Anne slipping.

The first time I really knew we had big problems was when I wasn't willing to sign for a Pell Grant loan for her to go to hairdressing school. I wasn't willing to sign because she would have been in school six nights a week for two years. I thought she should go during the day five days a week for eight months instead. She complained that we only had one vehicle, and I suggested she take the bus on those days when I needed the car. Well, she equated my reasoning with trying to keep her down because she was a woman. I never understood why she thought that, but looking back, I realize I was selfish.

LESSON 24—BEING SELFISH AND CONTROLLING WILL GUARANTEE YOU A MISERABLE RELATIONSIIIP.

She was so angry that she screamed and cried, cussing at me for hours. She broke every dish in the house, smashing them one by one against the wall, screaming that I was trying to keep her down because she's a woman.

It got so bad that when I attempted to physically stop her, she equated that with abuse and she wasn't shy about letting the children know that was how she felt.

LESSON 25—NEVER INVOLVE YOUR CHILDREN IN A SPOUSAL DISAGREEMENT. IT IS ESPECIALLY IMPORTANT NEVER TO MISLEAD IN ORDER TO GAIN THEIR FAVOR.

Towards the end of my tour in Hawaii, I decided to surprise her for her twenty ninth birthday. I invited all of our friends over, and bought her a nice sweater for $75.00. While opening my gift in front of everyone she said "Nice going genius, a sweater in Hawaii?" I was embarrassed, and hurt.

LESSON 26—WHEN YOU RECEIVE A GIFT, SHOW YOUR APPRECIATION BOTH IN PUBLIC AND PRIVATE, WHETHER YOU ENJOY THE GIFT OR NOT.

I'm not implying that I was a model husband, because I wasn't by a long stretch. We were going in different directions and growing apart from each other. I focused too much on my military career and children and not enough on what should have been my top priority, my wife. Conversely, she was spreading her wings and reacted by criticizing everything I did. She blamed me for my knee injury that caused my abrupt discharge from the army and a complete change of life as we knew it.

After my discharge in September 1992, I had to decide what I was going to do with my life. We moved in with my mother-in-law in Florida until we could figure something out. It's hard enough living under someone else's roof, let alone someone who absolutely despises you, but that's exactly what I did.

I got off on the wrong foot right from the beginning. My mother-in-law was not as tidy as I would have liked. If I was going to be living there for any amount of time, I figured the place needed to be cleaned up and I would do it. In my mind I thought I was doing a good thing, but that's not how "Mrs. Johnson", (as I always called her), took it. She was extremely offended and she had every right to be. After all, who was I to enter her home and immediately start turning things inside out like I was spring-cleaning?

LESSON 27—WHEN YOU STAY UNDER SOMEONE ELSE'S ROOF, YOU LIVE BY THEIR RULES, NOT YOURS.

In fact, she told me if I didn't like it, I should get the hell out of her house. That's what I did.

I got a job working and living in a funeral home in Miami, which was a three-hour drive from where we were staying. We decided that I would relocate to Miami while attending Mortuary College while Mary Anne and the kids remained with her mother in Melbourne. I was working for six bucks per hour and going to school full-time in Miami while Mary Anne was going to school for medical assistant training and working full time as well in Melbourne.

Good plan, right? Disaster is more like it. The fact is, living apart while married simply doesn't work. You would think I learned my lesson from this experience, but I turned around and did the exact same thing seventeen years later with my second wife, with the same result, divorce.

LESSON 28—LEARN FROM YOUR MISTAKES. FAILURE TO DO SO ALLOWS PAST PROBLEMS TO HAUNT YOU.

I was trying to put my life back together, yet it seemed to be unraveling at the same time. Mary Anne wasn't happy with our circumstances, and I can't say that I blame her. We were very comfortable living in Hawaii in Senior NCO (Non Commissioned Officer) quarters. Now we were apart, poor, and not living in our own home.

The daily grind started to wear on her. She mentioned to me, on more than one occasion, how much it had sucked to have nothing. She hated our life and couldn't see any light at the end of the tunnel.

It became depressing to hear all the negative things. In the meantime, I was doing well in school and getting a lot of attention from some very beautiful younger women who I thought appreciated me more. It turns out they didn't appreciate anything. However, after thirteen years of being completely faithful in every aspect of my marriage, I finally sinned. I loved the attention, but I was only digging my hole deeper and deeper with each day. It was no fun trying to live two lives.

LESSON 29—OH, THE TANGLED WEBS WE WEAVE WHEN FIRST WE PRACTICE TO DECEIVE.

We somehow managed to stay together. One reason was that I never admitted my infidelities, the other was the affect I thought divorce would have on my children. Mary Anne threw me out of the house while I was interning as a Funeral Director in Florida. I was ready to file for divorce when my son Joey (seven at the time) called me on the phone. He was crying and begged me to come back home. Against my better judgment, I begged and pleaded with Mary Anne to take me back. I had never kissed anyone's ass so much in my life, but it was for my kids' sake. It was over then. I should have accepted that and moved on. The remaining year and a half left in my marriage was hell.

LESSON 30—NEVER STAY TOGETHER SOLELY FOR THE KIDS' SAKE.

We ended up moving back to New England where I got a job as a Funeral Director/Embalmer in New Hampshire. I thought it would be a fresh start, and hoped that what had happened in Florida was forgotten. Life doesn't work that way. Our problems seemed to mount with every day.

LESSON 31—CHANGING GEOGRAPHICAL LOCATIONS DOES NOT CHANGE THE PROBLEM. IT JUST CHANGES THE LOCATION OF THE PROBLEM.

Things went from bad to worse, and we divorced in 1996. When divorce happens, you don't just divorce your spouse. This situation put me in the doghouse with Mary Anne's entire family, including Uncle Jerry and Aunt Pat, who I absolutely adored. It was a very difficult loss for me, but one I deserved.

LESSON 32—DIVORCE AFFECTS MUCH MORE THAN THE TWO PEOPLE NAMED IN THE DECREE.

I am thankful, however, that Mary Anne found it in her heart to remain friendly to me. She has since moved on and she's happier than I ever could have made her.

CHAPTER 5

School Years

As I mentioned in a previous chapter, my time spent in school was boring, difficult and miserable. A few things happened in my junior high and high school days, however, that I'd like to mention.

Teachers simply hated me. I was such an asshole that I would have hated me too. Because I never got attention at home, other than the negative kind, I felt compelled to be class clown in order to gain favor with my fellow students. Most of the students laughed, but the teachers didn't find me so amusing.

Eighth grade civics class at Higgins Jr. High in Peabody, Mass., had the coolest teacher in the state. Everybody loved Mr. Gilligan. He was young, handsome, athletic and very popular with the students.

One day I decided I was going to make a joke about the shirt he was wearing in front of the entire class. The class laughed all right, but I found myself standing outside in the hallway during class for the entire week. My antics didn't stop there and I left quite an impression on Mr. Gilligan that year.

Looking over my junior high yearbook a few years ago, I noticed a nice little inscription written on the autograph page by Mr. Gilligan. It read, "Eric, if you find time to play in traffic this summer, please do. Or perhaps try skydiving, anything that puts your life in a threatening situation". Obviously, Mr. Gilligan hated me. To this day I've been trying to track him down to apologize, and show him I ended up okay, not that he'd remember me, but for my own peace of mind.

LESSON 33—SOMEONE WILL REMEMBER THE THINGS YOU SAY AND DO. BEFORE YOU SAY OR DO ANYTHING, ASK YOURSELF, "WILL I REGRET THIS?"

There was the time in seventh grade in Mr. Lawless's geography class that I thought I would show off by swearing at people in Portuguese. Well, Maria Afonso, a fellow student and native of Portugal, wasn't going to stand for my foul mouth. She warned me twice never to say it again, but do you think I listened?

After I said something in Portuguese (I still don't know what it meant. I think it was something on a woman's anatomy), she promptly picked up a chalk eraser and repeatedly slapped it in my face. By the time she was done, my face looked like I got run over with a million erasers. I sat in my seat dumbfounded and shocked.

It wasn't until my twentieth class reunion that I got the opportunity to apologize to Maria for what I did twenty-six years earlier. I was walking around to each table selling 50/50 tickets and saw her nametag. I thought I would tell her my story.

I said, "I have to apologize for something I did in seventh grade". She replied "I don't even know you. What do you mean?" I said, "Well one day in Mr. Lawless's class I learned how to swear in Portuguese". She immediately put her hands to her face, and said, "Oh my God, That was you?!" she said, "I am so embarrassed!". I said, "No, I'm embarrassed, and I'm sorry for what I did." She accepted my apology, and I was able to enjoy the rest of the evening.

LESSON 34—DON'T DO ANYTHING THAT YOU WILL HAVE TO APOLOGIZE FOR AT YOUR CLASS REUNION.

High school wasn't much better. There wasn't so much clowning around, but lots of fighting. I was encouraged to us my fists whenever necessary. So I did. I think I broke the record at Peabody High for being suspended the most times for fighting in a three-year period.

There were many memorable battles. Today, those battles would have found me behind bars. There was one fight in particular where I told my father a kid was talking trash to me. This one really stands out in my mind. After the fight, I got suspended for a week because two teachers got injured trying to break it up. I got so tired of that high school and my bad grades that I asked to be transferred to vocational school. At first, my father agreed, but the next morning when I woke up to start at the vocational school, my father had a change of heart.

You see I was taking the easy way out. I thought the vocational school was for dumber kids (I was wrong again). My father knew that and decided to wait until he was in a really foul mood the next morning to let me know it.

I remember wearing an Irish knit sweater and overalls when I came down the stairs that day. He told me I wasn't going to the VOC and I'd better get my ass back upstairs and change into something decent before he took me back to high school.

Before I could get to the stairs, however, he grabbed me by the throat and threw me up against the wall. While squeezing my throat, he screamed at me that he didn't want me working for a certain type of people my whole life. His prejudice was ridiculous, but his passion for my success was very real.

He figured if I went to the VOC, I would be working for "The Man" my entire life. Well, I didn't go to the VOC and I still work for "The Man". In fact, most VOC graduates who learned a trade are in far more demand than I am and they're making more money as well.

LESSON 35—AN EDUCATION IS AN EDUCATION, VOCATIONAL OR OTHERWISE. DON'T KNOCK IT.

He wrote a letter to my unit director, Mr. Eager, and told me to give it to him when I got to school. Now I was dressed in my Sunday best while my father drove to the high school on the day I thought my life was going to get easier. He pulled up to the main doors of the high school, slammed on his brakes, screeched, and skidded for a couple of feet and yelled at me to get the fuck out. There I was walking to the high school doors getting all kinds of stares from all the girls who were smoking outside. Talk about embarrassing! The letter my father wrote was sealed and I didn't dare look at it. I brought it to Mr. Eager. He read it and told me to go to class. To this day, I don't know what the letter said.

I never really knew my place in high school. I was never smart enough, good looking enough or had the personality to attract anyone. The only thing I was good at was work, my paper route, my chores at home and my part-time job.

I did learn responsibility at an early age. I paid room and board since I was thirteen. I paid to do my own laundry at the house because my father installed a coin-operated washing machine. He insisted I get my own life insurance at age fifteen because as he said, "I don't have money to pay for a pine box when you die".

Maybe my father didn't exactly have the best methodology in teaching me how to be responsible, but it did work.

LESSON 36—EVERY ADOLESCENT SHOULD BE MADE TO PAY SOMETHING TOWARDS ROOM AND BOARD. EVEN IF YOU PUT THE MONEY IN THE BANK FOR THEM, MAKE THEM PAY.

School was a different matter, however. I think because my parents had six kids and they both worked full time, they didn't take the opportunity to check on our progress in school. This only made it easier for me to screw off. I could have cared less about my grades. I was one of those clock-watchers just waiting for each class to end.

I never realized how important it was for me to do well in high school. If I had known then what I know now, I would have gone for straight A's and become a doctor. Instead, I was shooting for a C and considered myself very fortunate to be a funeral director. It could have been a lot worse for me, but I simply didn't know any better.

LESSON 37—YOUTH IS WASTED ON THE YOUNG.

When I was in high school, the only things important to me were girls, fighting and showing off. I don't know what my GPA was, but my average grade in four years of high school was 70%. I was so happy to have graduated, even though I had to go to summer school after my senior year to make up three credits because I had too many F's. It was no fun staying home on graduation day while all my friends got to walk across the stage and get their diplomas. I remember sitting alone in my room just crying because I felt so bad for myself. Like they say, I made my own bed.

LESSON 38—WE REAP WHAT WE SOW.

Thank God for the U.S. Army.

CHAPTER 6

The Army

The United States Army molded me into the man I am today. There is no other institution in the world that could have done for me what the army did. I expected to do my three years, get what I wanted out of them and then go on my merry way. Instead, I re-enlisted two more times and had more experiences than I ever could have imagined. Soldiering was my thing.

It wasn't all easy, and it certainly didn't start out that way. In fact, on day two when we got our hair buzzed off, I was ready to go home. I hated every second of basic training. I was just getting used to my freedom from my parents and I volunteered to be treated like shit all over again.

I remember when the bus pulled up to the Ft. Dix reception station filled with young kids from all over the country. During the entire drive from Newark Airport to Ft. Dix, all we did was screw around just like any group of young kids would. We were laughing and bullshitting and having a grand old time.

Then the first drill sergeant I ever saw entered the bus. He was so nice. He welcomed all of us to the United States Army, told us how proud he was of us for volunteering and assured us we would be well taken care of during our tenure at Ft. Dix. It all felt so warm and fuzzy, nothing like the horror stories our grandfathers told us about when they were in the service. This was going to be a piece of cake. The drill sergeant finished his speech, once again welcoming us with open arms. Then all of a sudden, the guy went berserk! Screaming at the top of his lungs, he instructed us in very unpleasant terms to get off the bus immediately, if not sooner.

We ran off that bus, tripping all over each other. When we got off, we were supposed to line up in formation (we didn't even know what the hell a formation was), with our suitcases. Well, nobody had the right suitcase because the other drill sergeants threw them all in one pile and they had only given us ten seconds to get off the bus, get our suitcases and be in formation. Drill sergeants also count a little different than the rest of us. They count backwards from 10 and it sounds something like this: "ten, nine, eight, seven, three, two, one FREEZE!" They always left out a few seconds, but we weren't going to argue.

I made it through basic training relatively easy, but certainly not the top recruit in the class. Then it was off to Ft. Gordon, GA for Advanced Individual Training, better known as A.I.T. Ft. Gordon was where the communication schools in the army were located. After three months of A.I.T, it was off to my first permanent party duty station, the infamous Ft. Bragg, N.C.

Every nut in the military was stationed at Ft. Bragg. The second largest post in the country (behind Ft. Ord, CA), Ft. Bragg was the home of the 18th Airborne Corps, 82nd Airborne Division, Fifth, and Seventh Special Forces and the U.S. Army Special Operations Command, which included Delta Force Headquarters and the Army Special Forces (Green Berets) Training Center. They were the best of the best and the craziest of the crazies.

I ended up in the 50th Signal Battalion, which was part of the 35th Signal Brigade, and 18th Airborne Corps. I got to the unit as a leg, (a non-airborne troop), who were considered pieces of shit by all of the paratroopers. Boy did it suck being a nasty leg amongst all those elite paratroopers. I went to Airborne School at Ft. Benning, GA, as soon as there was an opening. I was proud as a peacock when I returned to my unit with wings on my chest and a maroon beret. I called my dad and said, "Dad, I got my maroon beret and I am a paratrooper now." Instead of congratulating me and being happy, he said, "When are you going to get the real one?" meaning the Green Beret of the Special Forces.

LESSON 39—SHOW YOUR PRIDE TO YOUR CHILDREN FOR THEIR ACCOMPLISHMENTS, WHETHER LARGE OR SMALL. WHAT YOU THINK TO THEM MATTERS MORE THAN WHAT YOU THINK TO YOURSELF.

When I first got to Bragg, I really didn't know a damn thing. My boots were clean and brush shined, but I never learned how to spit shine until later. Basic Leadership Course changed everything for me. By the time I graduated from BLC, my shoes looked like mirrors, my uniforms were highly pressed, my hair was high and tight and I knew how to carry myself like a real paratrooper. I graduated as the 2nd Honor Graduate and was the recipient of the Leadership Award. For the very first time in my life, I proved to myself that I could do anything I set my mind to and that I wasn't the dummy I always thought I was. I was given the chance and I took it.

LESSON 40—DON'T BE AFRAID TO TAKE RISKS. YOU CAN'T STEAL SECOND BASE IF YOU KEEP YOUR FOOT ON FIRST.

I trained with some real crazy bastards at Bragg. My platoon was TACCP (Tactical Command Post). We were the front line communicators for the Commander of the 18th Airborne Corps a Three Star General. We all knew we were the misfits of the battalion. We and everybody else also knew we were the best communicators in the army. Still, the guys in the platoon were like brothers.

Sergeant First Class David K. Frazee led us. Mark Buddenhagen (Bud), Tom Gardner, David Cushing, Jerry Thomason, Cornelius Cousins, Eric Link, John Lonsberry, Jon Weigman, Augustine Papillo, Dennis Pope, Matthew Clarke, Herman Thompson, John Liemieux, Kenny Roberts, Leonard Robinson (Ranger Rob), Rob Holden, Rich Danko, Robert Taylor, Clyde Collins, Joe Provenzano, Eric Duran, Todd Gilmore, Kendall Kilbourn, Patrick McNerney,

Carl Bowyer, Freddie Rodriguez, Grant Gillen, Richard Carpenter, Sheldon Schultz, Wade Miller, Melvin Eckardt, Robert Meurer, and others, made up the platoon.

The army had names to every operation, whether real world or just an exercise, i.e.: "Operation Just Cause" in Panama, "Desert Storm" in the Gulf. One mission I recall very well was "Bright Star 1983" in Egypt.

I really appreciated being in the U.S. Army when I saw how the Egyptian Army lived. Our unit did a parachute jump with them and some of their paratroopers didn't even have bootlaces. This was their elite! Afterwards, we all got together to trade items. One American got a nice shiny pair of Egyptian Jump Wings in exchange for a lousy nail clipper.

LESSON 41—ONE MAN'S JUNK IS ANOTHER MAN'S TREASURE.

The heat was blistering during the day and windy and cold at night. The homemade field latrines were nothing more than a ditch with plywood. There were six holes to each large sheet of plywood, so it wasn't uncommon to be doing your thing with five other guys doing theirs in full view of each other. The army never gave a rat's ass about privacy. I showered by punching holes in a coffee can and hanging the can on a camouflage net pole. Conditions were less than adequate, shall we say, so it gave me a great appreciation for what I had back home.

LESSON 42—IF YOU THINK YOUR LIFE IS DIFFICULT, LIVE IN THE SHOES OF SOMEONE FROM A THIRD WORLD COUNTRY. YOU'LL HAVE A GREATER APPRECIATION FOR THE UNITED STATES.

Honduras was another place that opened my eyes to how the rest of the world lived. I ended up on the top of a place called "Tiger Island". It was very remote, and it took a helicopter to get from the bottom, called Amapala, to the top. It was my three-man paratrooper team, and a battalion full of marines. We all got along great. The marines introduced me to the two stray dogs on the island, which became their mascots. They named them Penis and Anus. It was an interesting tour with interesting people, but I don't think I'll be visiting Honduras anytime soon.

The day we returned from Egypt, we were worn out and ready to crash in a real bed after a real shower. I lived in a six-man room with other paratroopers. While trying to sleep, we heard a drunk outside screaming at the top of his lungs, something about his mother. Apparently, this jerk got into an argument with another soldier when the other guy said something derogatory about the jerk's mother.

We all awoke at 1AM listening to this guy continue to go on and on about beating up anyone who talked about his mother. We were on the second floor of the barracks and could hear him outside, clear as a bell. We asked him to simmer down and go to bed, but to no avail. Finally, after listening to this guy continue to go on about his mother, we opened the window, showed him a book we were holding, and my friend, Sergeant Phillip Wimp (now a police officer in Michigan) said, "Hey Asshole, you know what the title of this book is? 'Your Momma in Five Easy Steps'!"

This guy went crazy. He actually climbed up to the second floor ledge where we helped him through the window into our room and proceeded to beat him silly.

LESSON 43—PICK THE HILL YOU WANT TO DIE ON CAREFULLY. SOMETIMES IT'S WISER TO WALK AWAY.

My three years at Ft. Bragg came and went pretty fast. I thought going to Panama was going to be great. Panama ended up being the worst three years in the army for two reasons. One was the corrupt government and the unfriendly people, and the other was the miserable people I worked for when I was in Bravo Company 154th Signal Battalion at Ft. Clayton.

I was a very young sergeant and was at the top of my game when I got there. Coming from Ft Bragg, I suppose I was a bit cocky, but I don't think I really showed it. I ended up in a newly formed company with some hateful and jealous people.

Like anything in life, there will be people that won't like you because you have succeeded in areas that they have not, or as in the army, you got promoted earlier than they did. Day one in Panama showed me I was going to have to work really hard to please some of these guys.

There always was, and I suppose there always will be, issues with blacks and whites. We got along because we had to, but there was no love lost between most of us. I was treated like I was stupid, as if they were so much better than me. These guys were good at what they did, they were in great shape, and they no doubt earned their way, but so did I. It was the first time in my life that I was in the minority and the first time I was discriminated against. The platoon sergeant I had was not my biggest fan.

Any chance he got to punish me or make me look bad, he took it. This guy was a low-life bottom feeder who happened to find his way in the army and ended up retiring after he put in his twenty years. For the year I was in his platoon, he made me hate life.

A sergeant first-class makes decent money and lives in nice on-base housing for free. This guy didn't own a car, so he purchased a used moped. He would putt-putt to work in his moped wearing his Kevlar army helmet because he couldn't afford a real motorcycle helmet. Every white guy in the platoon hated his guts.

He had a terrible under bite and looked just like a Piranha. He would yell at the platoon and drool down his chin. We made fun of him when he threw his temper tantrums by asking each other when he was going to jump out of his fish bowl.

I guess my point bringing this guy up is to illustrate how much we all affect the people we live and work with daily. I was twenty-two years old when this all went on and I only remember what a rotten piece of shit this guy was.

LESSON 44—A PERSON MAY NOT ALWAYS REMEMBER ALL THE KIND PEOPLE HE COMES IN CONTACT WITH, BUT HE WILL REMEMBER THE MEAN PEOPLE. DON'T BE MEAN.

I did have quite a few adventures with the military in Panama. One of them was a 63-mile road march from the Atlantic side of Panama to the Pacific side. We had our rucksacks full and plenty of water, but it wasn't easy.

About twenty miles into the road march, we ran into a pack of Howler Monkeys. Someone threw a rock at them. Being territorial, they retaliated. We all ran like hell until they stopped chasing us. When we bedded down for the night a few hours later, these wild monkeys pelted us with rocks. We learned to leave the monkeys alone after that.

In September of 1986, I went through the toughest training I have ever faced. It was called Pana-Jungla (pronounced Pana-Hungla) School. It was the most difficult survival course in the Western Hemisphere. The chief instructor was none other than "Pineapple Face" himself, the infamous General Manuel Antonio Noriega.

The reason I volunteered for this training was because every soldier I asked about it said they wouldn't send their worst enemy. There were true stories of guys ending up in the hospital and even someone dying as a result of the rigorous and very dangerous training. To me that was a challenge, and I never back away from a challenge.

Just to qualify for this school, we had to take a physical fitness test that went far beyond the scope of the P.T. test the U.S. Army offered. This was a course from a foreign country and you played by their rules. We had to do fifty perfect pushups in one minute, sixty sit-ups in one minute, a one-mile run in boots in less than six minutes and thirty seconds, and a half-mile swim with full gear in the ocean.

The Panamanian Defense Forces were small and corrupt, but their elite troops ran the Pana-Jungla school and they were the best jungle experts in the world. The U.S. Army had what was called the JOTC (Jungle

Operations Training Center) on Ft. Sherman in Panama where they trained Americans throughout the army. After graduating from JOTC, one was awarded the distinction of being a jungle expert. In fact, the patch authorized to wear on your uniform said just that, "Jungle Expert". The truth is, you were no more of a Jungle Expert after graduating from JOTC than you were a NASCAR expert once you obtained a driver's license. The coveted Pana-Jungla Badge, however, was a different story. When people saw that badge on your uniform, you were revered.

I already knew going in that I wasn't going to see much food for the entire four-week course. We ate what we killed and we shared it as a class. So, the night before I left for training, I ate the best steak dinner I ever had. The next day when we left for the remote regions of Panama near the Costa Rican border, the hell began.

We went from a bus to a truck, to a boat, to a tractor, to humping the last ten miles in our boots. It took two days to get there and all they gave us for food was one cheese sandwich. When I bit into the sandwich, it was hard to chew. That's when I realized they left the plastic wrap on the cheese after making the sandwich. It was food, and I ate it.

The first day found us being stripped of everything we had. No canteen, water, rucksack, food, nothing. We were taught how to make a canteen, a knife, a fork, a spoon and a bowl out of bamboo. The only instruments we had to work with were a machete and a small pocketknife.

We also learned how to build a waterproof shelter from the natural elements of the jungle and a fire pit with cover to go along with our shelter. We were graded on everything we did. To graduate, you needed a minimum of eight hundred points out of a perfect score of one thousand. Eighty-four soldiers, both American, and Panamanian, started the course. Twenty-two men stood for graduation, and eleven of us were actually awarded the badge. I always felt bad for the poor bastards that made it all the way through only to find out at graduation that they didn't have enough points to graduate. For the record, I graduated with eight hundred and two points. I made it by the skin of my teeth.

After a few days, the instructors decided to be nice and offer a half of a piece of bologna to anyone who could climb a very thick forty-foot rope. By the time I got to the rope, it was wet, muddy, and as slippery as ice. I made it about five feet up the rope and just didn't have the strength to go any further. After coming down, I had to go in a sandpit filled with fire ants and do fifty push-ups with all the other guys who didn't make it up to the top. We had to watch the guys that did make it eat their piece of bologna. It was humiliating and it made me even hungrier. So, the next day when we got the same offer, I was so hungry there wasn't anything that was going to stop me from getting to the top, not even watching the guy before me make it to the top, only to let go from weakness. He splattered on the ground in front of me. The Panamanian instructors simply kicked him out of the way so we could continue. Needless to say, I made it to the top without a problem and thoroughly enjoyed my little piece of bologna.

LESSON 45—THE HUMAN MIND IS INCREDIBLE. NEVER UNDERESTIMATE ITS CAPABILITIES.

About two weeks into the class, we were really starving. A couple of pieces of bologna a week and the meager helpings of monkey and other jungle wildlife that we killed weren't exactly cutting it. They gave us a block of instructions on how to find an edible bush branch. The whole branch wasn't edible, but you could bite into it and suck some of the juice it contained.

Later that day when we were chopping grass with our machetes, I noticed a bush nearby I thought was the edible kind they had just taught us about. We all, (about ten of us), went over to check it out. Once we knew it was the edible bush, all hell broke loose. It was every man for himself and a classic example of survival of the fittest. It got so bad that one American started swinging his machete at another over a twig. I watched in amazement while one guy literally tried to kill his fellow comrade out of hunger. People will do just about anything when they're starving.

In fact, a few days after that, the instructors got us into formation and handed each of us the biggest, most beautiful bananas we had ever seen. They gave each of us one banana with the stipulation that we would have another formation at midnight and we had to have our bananas unpeeled and uneaten at that formation. At that point, I asked what would happen if we didn't have the banana on us. The instructor told us we would lose ten points. I immediately peeled my banana and ate it on the spot. I figured, "Take points? I've got to stay alive here". Subsequently, at midnight formation, all those guys who had their bananas got them taken away just so the instructors could screw with their heads.

LESSON 46—TAKE OPPORTUNITIES WHEN THEY ARE PRESENTED TO YOU, BECAUSE THE FUTURE IS UNCERTAIN.

Just about everybody tried to smuggle in some type of food on day one, including yours truly. Since they let us keep toothpaste and shampoo, I emptied my see-through shampoo bottle ahead of time, and filled it with honey. It probably saved my life. The first week I was dabbing the honey on my fingers and licking them. By week three, I was guzzling it. I made it a point to share anything I had with my fellow students. We were all in this together and I never even gave it a second thought not to share. I was very disappointed to discover that I was the exception. There were guys hoarding stuff that they would just as soon die over than share. Every single guy who refused to share any food didn't graduate.

LESSON 47—SELFISH MEN END UP LOSING SOONER OR LATER.

I got a little selfish myself when I decided to eat my toothpaste. Much like the honey, I dabbed some on my finger just to be able to taste something. I was so hungry that I literally swallowed half the tube of Colgate. I was sick to my stomach for days.

Graduation was really strange. We killed a goat and hung it upside down in the center of our living area. We then placed a bucket under his head and slit his throat until the blood poured in the bucket. The day before, we killed some wild dogs and put their hearts in the bucket of goat's blood.

Noriega called us up one by one and we were to go up to the goat, bite the dog's heart, wash our face with the goat's blood, then we were to post in front of General Noriega so he could shake our hands and hand us our diploma. We were hungry, tired, and delusional, so we did what we were told. Noriega ate it up. He had blood dripping from his hands with a huge smile on his face. Graduating from Pana-Jungla School was the one thing I am most proud of in my life. I learned not only about survival, but also about human nature, suffering, starving, and mostly I learned about myself. I kept my temptations in check and I made it.

LESSON 48—TEMPTATION RESISTED IS THE TRUE MEASURE OF CHARACTER.

I got promoted to staff sergeant while I was in Panama and I had the opportunity to play goalkeeper on the U.S. Army South soccer team. However, I was tickled to death to leave that place and looked forward to enjoying whatever adventures lay ahead in Hawaii.

Hawaii truly is God's country. The weather is perfect, the land is beautiful, the people are friendly, the food is delicious, and the entertainment is phenomenal. Too bad I wasn't there on vacation. I was fortunate enough to be stationed there from 1988-1992. Even though it was a tour of duty, it was like a vacation every day when I wasn't working.

I became the platoon sergeant for DTAC platoon. DTAC is the acronym for Divisional Tactical Communications. Much like TACCP at Ft. Bragg, we were the front line communicators for the 25th Infantry Division. Normally, an E-7 (sergeant first class) would fill the platoon sergeant slot, but I got picked by the battalion commander to do it as an E-6 (staff sergeant). Although I eventually got promoted to E-7, there were some bad feelings with some of the E-7's in a lower position. I can't say that I blamed them.

We had a platoon leader; who was a short stocky black guy with an ego that couldn't fit in a freight car. He was buddy-buddy with all the black guys in the platoon and it made my job very difficult. He would undermine everything I said. One of his buddies was a tall, arrogant and very prejudiced black guy.

This guy was a thorn in my side. He acted like he was tough, but he was all mouth. Anytime he disagreed with me, he'd go running to the lieutenant. One day when we were on an exercise on the Big Island, and this arrogant soldier pushed me a little too far. I got up at about two in the morning and calmly walked to his shelter where he was on shift. I asked him to step outside so we could settle our differences like men, but he predictably backed down. He had the nerve the next day to tell all his buddies that I went to him and talked to him "like a bitch". I really wanted to give this guy a beat down.

I was very lucky that my subordinate backed down the night I challenged him. If he had taken me up on my challenge, I very well could have gotten demoted. I let my emotions get the best of me, and it could have ended up in a disaster.

LESSON 49—WHEN YOU LET YOUR EMOTIONS OVERCOME YOUR REASONING, YOU MAKE YOURSELF UNREASONABLE.

DTAC was still a great platoon. The guys were very similar to the other men when I was a private in TACCP, but this time I was the platoon sergeant. We even challenged an entire company to a relay involving physical fitness and military tasks. Our eighteen-man platoon held our own and only lost by less than a minute. Not bad versus a sixty-four man company.

During my time in Hawaii and throughout my career in the army, I received seven Army Achievement Medals, one Army Commendation Medal, one Meritorious Service Medal, the Air Assault Badge, the Airborne Badge, the Pana-Jungla Badge, Three Good Conduct Medals, promotion to E-7, two 25th Infantry Division Masters Badges and acceptance to both Officers Candidate School and White House Communications. The two most rewarding accomplishments, however, were graduating from P.O.W. Life in Captivity Course and being selected to train with the Brits and Gurkhas in Hong Kong.

P.O.W School was a trip. We signed a form prior to the beginning of the course that said we understand it was a "Hands-On" course. They didn't tell us it was their hands on us.

We attended three days of classroom instruction on various topics which one might face in a P.O.W camp, including how to resist interrogation. The instructors were nice guys from a military intelligence battalion on our post. We learned the prisoner of war tap code, ways to kill time, how to keep out of trouble, how to survive and how to work together as a team. The plan was that after the three days of instruction, the role-playing would begin where the students became prisoners, and the instructors became the captors.

They started by "capturing" us and putting hoods over our heads. They loaded us in the back of a five-ton truck and drove us out to a remote location. When we arrived, they laid us on the ground on our stomachs until we were kicked as a signal to get up.

We ended up in a large cave where they stripped us naked, gave us bottoms and tops and took away our socks. They took the laces out of our boots and had us walking around in them with hoods on our heads all day.

Their rules were outrageous. First, they insisted we were criminals, not prisoners of war. They gave us a number and asked us to repeat what number we were. I, for example, was criminal number twenty-two. So when they asked me who I was, I replied, "Sir, I am criminal number twenty-two, sir". The captor was happy and I didn't get slapped around.

I can't say the same for a younger soldier who insisted to be called a prisoner rather than a criminal. Our "captors" didn't take too kindly to this young man's stubborn ways and thus made sure we all got aptly punished for quite a long while. I was so relieved when the kid finally gave in so we could stop doing push ups and flutter kicks after two hours!

LESSON 50—STUBBORNESS DESTROYS REASONING MORE THAN YOUR EMOTIONS DO.

We never knew when the course was going to end or what day or time it was. We never slept and were kept in caves much of the time. If we weren't getting slapped around, we were doing hard labor. They soaked us down with water, then made us low crawl in sand. It was so uncomfortable with all the sand down your pants and in your nose and ears. The whole idea for them was to make us as miserable as they could, while we were to stay working together at all costs.

They even told us during training that they were going to do this to us and we still let it get to us. While captive, they would tell us that our SRO (senior ranking officer) had said certain things. Our natural reaction was to be pissed at our SRO, because we believed what we were being told. After the course was over and we were getting debriefed, the instructors explained to us that they did lie to us so that we would not cooperate with or believe our SRO. It worked perfectly and we fell for it hook, line and sinker.

LESSON 51—BE CALM AND THINK THINGS THROUGH WHEN FACED WITH A LARGE AMOUNT OF STRESS. DO NOT MAKE IMPETUOUS DECISIONS.

For security purposes I'm not at liberty to discuss everything that went on in prisoner of war training. Suffice it to say, it was very realistic and very difficult.

I was fortunate to be one of twelve soldiers from the 25th Infantry Division selected to train in Hong Kong with the British Army and the Gurkhas. The Gurkhas were soldiers from Nepal, who the British Government hired to supplement their army. I always thought of them as trained mercenaries for the Brits. They were all little guys, but tough as nails. They could put a two hundred pound rucksack on their back, and walk up a mountain easier than you and I walk around the block. They were true killing machines and it was an honor to have had the privilege to train so closely with them. Off duty, they were great guys.

The British Army had so many wonderful people in it that I remain friends with many of them today. The English, the Scots and the Welsh all had their little rivalries, but they worked very well together as an army.

Training was interesting, but I found the nightlife in Hong Kong even better. When we had the opportunity for R&R, we took it. One night, we all ended up at a club called "The Pussy Cat Lounge". It was a normal club with a DJ just like you would see in the U.S. Well, my British buddies cajoled me into drinking to the point that I couldn't even see straight.

We caught a taxi at about 3am. I sat in the front seat with the driver and my three British buddies sat in the back. Apparently, I was being very loud and it irritated the taxi driver. He said something in Chinese to my buddies, one of whom spoke fluent Mandarin Chinese. I asked them what he said and they told me he had said I was too loud and it was bothering him. In my drunken state I wasn't about to take that crap. So, I made this really loud karate scream, "HI-AH!" and put my hands in front of me like I was Bruce Lee. Then I said, "OOH OOH" in a high voice while moving my hands up and down right in this guy's face. He pulled over and kicked us out of the taxi. My friend's attempts at explaining that I was just a crazy American fell on deaf ears and we ended up walking six miles home.

LESSON 52—WHEN YOU GET DRUNK, YOU LOSE CONTROL OF WHO YOU ARE. NEVER LOSE CONTROL.

Another incident happened on the two-minute ferry ride from the Hong Kong side of Victoria Harbor to the Kowloon side. Someone had a heart attack when the ferry was in the middle of the harbor. This was 1990 when cell phones were still a new thing and anyone carrying one was considered an important person. Luckily for the heart attack victim, there was a doctor on board. He asked if anyone had a cell phone and we pointed to a Chinese gentleman who was talking on one. When we told him to call an ambulance, he explained that the phone actually did not work. He was carrying it around and talking into it to no one, just so people would be impressed with him. What an asshole.

LESSON 53—NEVER TRY TO BE SOMEONE YOU ARE NOT. IF PEOPLE DON'T LIKE YOU FOR WHO YOU ARE, THEY'RE NOT WORTH BEING IN YOUR LIFE.

The training was intense, the friendships became life long, and the fun was unforgettable. That was my last mission in the army. I injured my knee severely while training there, which ended my military career with a medical discharge.

That's the point in my life when I decided I was going to mortuary school.

Chapter 7

College

Miami-Dade College had an excellent funeral program in the Philbrick School of Funeral Science. As mentioned previously, I landed a job and a place to live in a funeral home, while I attended school on a full-time basis.

I almost didn't go for fear that I wasn't quite smart enough to make it. It was a good thing I overcame that fear, because I forged great friendships and business relationships. I graduated top of my class as well as becoming President of the Miami Chapter of the National Morticians Honors Fraternity. It just goes to show if you don't try, you'll never know what you are capable of.

LESSON 54—THE GREATEST FAILURE IS THE FAILURE TO TRY.

Mortuary school was no cakewalk. In our anatomy class, the students were complaining to our professor that they had too much homework along with working full time and being on call every night. The professor had no mercy, although he did realize our loads were heavy. He told us he didn't want to hear any complaints because that's the way life is. He said if we wanted it bad enough, we would do it. In his words:

LESSON 55—YOU GOTTA DO WHAT YOU GOTTA DO!!!!

The first eight months of school were lonely ones. I didn't know anybody and I worked so much that I didn't have time to get to know anybody. I missed my wife and kids and all I did on my down time was think of them. Every evening I would just sit on my little twin bed in my one room efficiency above the embalming room and feel bad for myself. I would stare at the four walls with tears rolling down my face and second-guess every decision I made.

I studied for hours. To keep busy, I also did some tutoring in the classes I had completed. I got A's in those classes and I ended up having a group of students to tutor because I was the only one doing it for free. I also got involved with the honors fraternity after my first year once I started to establish some friendships.

My friend, Janis Taylor, and I were so poor. We had to combine our money in order to afford dinner. Our cars were junk boxes and we never had gas in the tanks. We did, however, have Islanda. Islanda is the name of a really cool calypso band that Janis introduced me to. We would go watch them every Thursday night at Bayside in Miami. Even when I had to study, I brought my schoolwork with me while I listened to the band. It definitely broke up the monotony.

LESSON 56—ALWAYS MAKE TIME FOR SOME LEISURE. WITHOUT IT, YOU BECOME EITHER DEPRESSED OR BORING.

The cast of characters in the funeral program were as varied as a bowl of mixed nuts (I emphasize the nuts). Although I was a good student, I clowned around a lot to bring some levity to the sometimes monotonous class work. Not everyone in each class graduated together because we were all on our own schedules. If we had the credits before graduation day, we graduated. If not, we continued on. There were always students coming and going throughout my two years at Miami Dade.

Towards the end of my program, I was taking a class called Funeral Directing. Since there was no prerequisite for this course, there were students in the class ready to graduate and others taking their very first class.

I was clowning around one day, and had the class, including the instructor, in stitches. I never disrupted the class, but when the opportunity presented itself, I took it. During the break, this guy approached me telling me how funny I was. I thanked him only to get a lecture. He told me I needed to get serious about my studies and when I get to be his age, I'll realize the importance of doing well in class.

I then asked him how old he was. He told me he was twenty-eight. I asked him if he had any children. He said he was married, but no children yet. I then asked him his GPA and he told me it was 2.8. I congratulated him (he had a total of six classes under his belt), and I thanked him for the advice, adding that I would be sure to work on it.

At that point, he asked me how old I was. I told him I was thirty. He asked me about children and I told him I had three. He asked me my GPA and I told him 3.67. I then added that I was graduating at the end of the semester and would be receiving the Outstanding Funeral Service Award, The Embalmers Technician Award for being the top embalmer in the class, and that I was going to be the student speaker at graduation. I was also awarded the Business Award for the entire college (not just funeral students), and was President of the funeral honors fraternity.

You should have seen this kid's mouth drop. Apparently, I was not only funny to him, but I looked and acted dumb as well. You know what this lesson is?

LESSON 57—DON'T JUDGE A BOOK BY ITS COVER.

The graduation was perfect. Actually, my speech was received by a standing ovation, and I had the honor of speaking on the same stage with Congresswoman Ross-Latinen from Florida. My professor, and friend, Ralph Covert, told me afterwards that it was beautiful. He said he was worried through the whole thing that I was going to come out with the F-word, because he knew it was my favorite. I explained to Ralph that I knew the difference between screwing around with the guys, and speaking in public to families and dignitaries. The only reason I did better than the others in the class was that I worked harder. There were so many students that were much brighter than I will ever be. I had to work harder than they did if I was to get any recognition at all.

LESSON 58—HARD WORK WILL BEAT TALENT UNLESS TALENT WORKS HARD.

CHAPTER 8

The Funeral Business

I've learned that things usually aren't as great as you imagined them. Funeral service is no exception. When I was a kid looking up to Ben Brodeur, my funeral director, and wondering how intriguing it would be to be in his shoes, I never considered the down side. I thought the upside was going to be so much better than it is.

Don't get me wrong, I love serving families and making a difference. Let's face it, everyone only gets one funeral and I'm the person you come to, to trust that the last thing you will ever do for your loved one is exactly how you (or they) want it. That's the good part. I'm also the one who you think is lying in wait to take all of your money, so all of your frustration gets taken out on me. You're sad and upset when you come in. You're not yourself because you can't think straight and the horror stories you've heard have you on guard against heartless money-grubbing bastards like me. That's the bad part.

Let's face it, it's a business and we are trying to make a living. I've noticed over the years that funeral directors and the funeral profession in general get a bad rap. Sometimes I feel like there's no sense in trying to defend or justify my position as a funeral director. If the NFDA (National Funeral Directors Association) hasn't been able to convince the public of anything, I certainly cannot. I can, however, share my stories and let the readers decide for themselves.

People get into the funeral business for one of two reasons. Either their family owns a funeral home and they intend on carrying on the family tradition, or they are like me and want to help people in their most difficult time. I have never met anybody in my fifteen years of doing this who came into it for the money. If they did, they didn't last long. That's because you can't make money in this business unless you are an owner or an executive in a corporation. Anyone who comes into funeral service for the money finds out quickly that somebody lied to him or her. Although I do ok, I'm far from wealthy. If you live in the real world, you would say that I make a decent living. The thing people don't understand is that the average funeral director lives a moderate life. As a manager, I was responsible for millions of dollars, thousands of human remains every year and several employees. Just handling complaints and avoiding lawsuits was a job in itself with such a large operation here in the state of Florida. A staff funeral director is farther down the fiscal chain. Again, it's a good living but you'll never, ever get rich. I do it because I want to do it.

LESSON 59—TO THINE OWN SELF BE TRUE.

Let's say you are enjoying your son's hockey game at 7pm Friday night, or your daughter's dance recital at 1pm Sunday afternoon, and someone dies. Your pager goes off. You must leave wherever you are, get in a suit and go immediately to pick the person up to bring them to your funeral home. If the person is to be embalmed, you must stay at the funeral home, embalm the body, and call the family for an arrangement time. Five hours gone right there. It generally takes two to three hours to embalm and about the same to get home, change and transfer the person from place of death to the funeral home. That's including phone calls and gathering the information you need legally to proceed.

If someone should die at 2am, you do the same thing, but you must look awake and refreshed in your suit when you go to the place of death. There's no shift work as in a hospital. Most funeral homes can't afford that kind of coverage, so the directors are all "On-call". Keep in mind, if we spend five hours in the middle of the night on a weeknight, we still have to report to the funeral home at 8am to work the next day. You work all day the next day and do the same thing that night. I pray at night before I go to bed that no one dies so I can get a good night's sleep, but most of the time my prayers fall on deaf ears.

You're at work the next day making arrangements in the morning with the family of the person you picked up the night before. When the arrangements are complete, the family leaves and you've got about another one or two hours of coordinating with clergy, newspapers, the health department, cemeteries, vault and casket companies and sometimes the VA. But before you get to that, you have to direct a funeral in early afternoon from a family two days prior. You return from the funeral, and immediately go to work on coordinating the arrangements you made that morning. In the meantime, vehicles need to be cleaned, rooms need to be vacuumed, bathrooms need scrubbing, and the family from the funeral wants you to deliver the ten left-over floral pieces to a local nursing home. While you're doing all this, someone else dies and it starts all over again.

Funeral directors don't just look pretty in a suit and drive big beautiful Cadillacs. We clean, paint, cut grass, trim bushes, plow snow, dust, vacuum, wash cars, visit with families, embalm, direct funerals and file more paperwork than we care to. The laws in place have us updating pricelists annually, getting inspected by the Federal Trade Commission, OSHA, and the state Embalmer's Board, (without notice), and paying exorbitant amounts in taxes, insurance and equipment mandated by the government.

We do all this and earn $5,500 (average) per funeral including the casket and vault. That's not $5,500 profit. We still must pay utilities, salary, wages, fixed and variable expenses and any unforeseen bills such as lawsuits or workman's comp. That $5,500 gets dwindled down quickly. Now, this happens with all businesses and there is a price to pay when you own or run a business. The difference is, when you buy a beautiful $3,000 Plasma T.V, you're happy. But because you put out $5,500 to bury your mom or dad, we in the funeral industry are often perceived as rotten people. I never understood how some people can spend four, five, six grand on TV's, stereos, computers, and other "toys" and still balk at what it costs to celebrate their loved ones life in a dignified and honorable manner. I just don't get it.

51

LESSON 60—HAVE YOUR PRIORITIES IN ORDER. IT'S NOT ALWAYS ALL ABOUT YOU.

I'd like to tell you another side of a funeral directors job. If you have a queasy stomach, please skip these next few paragraphs because there is no gentle way to describe death.

This is not a job for the weak stomach or mind. It is bloody, dirty, smelly, nasty and sad. We deal with elderly, middle age, teenagers and babies. We see heart attack victims, car wrecks, drowning victims, industrial accident victims, shooting victims and many people with contagious diseases. Death is not a pretty thing. In fact, before we can do our work, things start to happen to a dead body and decomposition begins immediately.

I have gone to pick people up who have died in their homes and were dead for days or even weeks before anyone noticed. I remember one gentleman in particular I picked up with another director at 1 AM on a hot summer night. When we turned the corner to the street of his residence, we immediately smelled a stench similar to a garbage truck. It was no surprise that the odor was coming from this man's bedroom.

He was on the second floor of a two-story apartment house and the woman who lived downstairs had just returned from vacation and called police when she discovered the smell. Of course, the maggots that had fallen from her ceiling and onto her kitchen counter gave it away. We entered the room trying to hold our breath. He was a big man and he was so far gone that he was completely black and unrecognizable.

While placing him in the pouch, I looked down only to see maggots all over my wingtips. I took five showers that night and bleached everything that he came in contact with. It took days to eliminate all the maggots from our stretcher and van.

I've gone into the middle of the woods in my suit to pick up people who have committed suicide using a gun. I've done this in the heat of summer, pouring rain and with snow up to my knees.

I will not get into the actual embalming procedure because this is not meant to be a technical chapter on embalming. Suffice it to say, it has its difficult moments. My point in describing these things is to help the average citizen understand what it is exactly that you are paying for. I'm sure no one reading this would want to do the gruesome tasks that I have described. That's just one reason things cost what they do.

More difficult than anything I've mentioned, is the emotional aspect of my job. Call my wife anytime and ask her how many nights I lay awake crying.

There was a one-week period, for example, that I handled the funerals of three children. One was a beautiful five-year-old girl who had been raped and suffocated to death. Another was a ten-year-old boy who died while tubing with his grandpa. The third one that week was a twelve-year-old girl who died from cancer.

The five-year-old was so precious. After embalming her, I kept trying to understand how anyone could do such a thing to such a beautiful baby. I wanted her hair perfect for her mom. My wife at the time, Kelly, came in to do her hair. She did a beautiful job. Trying to keep everything under control and comfort the baby's mom was very difficult. I had a job to do, but my feelings didn't go away.

The ten-year-old boy was my son Joey's age at that time and he was a handsome little guy. Naturally, I kept thinking of my son and how awful this was for the parents, especially the boy's grandpa. Apparently, his grandpa was driving the boat which was pulling the boy on a tube. They were on vacation and had a little cottage on the lake. Grandpa took a wide turn and the boy on the tube slammed into a wooden deck. He was killed instantly. I was so overcome with sadness I could barely embalm the kid.

The day after that, I went to a residence to pick up a twelve-year-old girl whom I met a couple of months earlier. She was lying in her bed holding onto her doll.

There are so many stories like these that I could write an entire book just on that. I did write a book describing the different ways I've been touched by the people I served called, "The Greatest People I Never Knew". It was written in a much different tone than this book, but it has wonderful stories about some very special people.

I explain all these things, not to whine or complain. I can hear some people reading this saying, "You picked the job, if you don't like it, get out." If you are one of those people, I would say you are right, except that I do like it, and I am staying. My whole point of this diatribe is that I, and everyone else in my profession, earn every penny we charge. In most cases, it's not up to par with what we deserve. Thus, the owners and corporations make the real money.

There are some lighter moments in our profession that deserve mentioning. It's not all doom and gloom. It is the natural order of life and we just happen to be the ones who are responsible for your final send-off.

At one funeral outside a Catholic church, the alarm on the hearse went off as the pallbearers were carrying the casket out of the church. There was no reason the alarm should have gone off and it was embarrassing for me. The family however, thought it was appropriate. They explained that the deceased gentleman was always impatient when he went to pick someone up at their house, so he'd lay on the horn until the person came out.

Another time, we were driving from New Hampshire to Massachusetts in a procession of three cars, my lead car, the limo, and the hearse. We were all trying to follow closely, but when we got on Route 1 in Saugas, Mass., we lost our hearse. The driver didn't see us because a garbage truck pulled in front of him. We went straight and the hearse pulled off at an exit and ended up in the parking lot of the local mall. We eventually called the hearse driver and got him to the cemetery, but when we got there, the family asked us what happened. When the driver explained what mall he ended up at, the family was convinced that the deceased woman had something to do with it. Since she lived in New Hampshire, she didn't get a lot of opportunity to visit her old neighborhood. So, when she did get to Massachusetts, she always made it a point to go to that particular mall where the hearse ended up. The family said she wanted to go shopping one last time before they laid her to rest.

Those two situations worked out perfectly for us at the funeral home when it could have been a disaster. There was the things that happen behind the scenes that no one sees but us.

One time I went to recon an old family cemetery site in the sticks of New Hampshire. The family gave me directions that led me to a dirt road. The dirt road led to a grass road that was obviously seldom used. I traveled the route the day before the funeral because the family wanted a procession to go all the way to the cemetery.

While driving on the grass road, I came upon a large rock sticking about six inches above the ground. This rock was in the middle of the road and I couldn't avoid it. When I drove over it, I scraped the bottom of the car on it and it tore the entire muffler off. I then found myself traveling down this unused road sounding like a Harley Davidson with new pipes. When I finally got to the end of the road, I had to exit the vehicle and walk through more woods to reach the little cemetery. As I was walking, this huge llama came out of nowhere and spat at me.

Being a city boy, I had no idea what to do, so I ran. This thing started chasing after me. I found myself running through woods in my suit trying to make it back to the car before this llama catches me. I did make it. Then, as I was driving back, the muffler got even louder and I ran into some bushes, which scratched the hell out of the car. I knew I was in deep shit when I finally got on a paved road and was able to assess the damage.

I spoke with the family the next day and the widow began laughing hysterically. I knew it was funny, but then she said to me, "That explains it." I said "Explains what?" she said, "The Chief of Police was out there looking for whoever was making all that noise." Apparently the people who owned the llamas must have heard me and called the police.

There was another time I was bringing a body to Logan Airport in Boston. It was a rainy night and it was difficult to see. When I got to what I thought was the Delta Cargo Terminal, they told me I was in the wrong place. Frustrated, I hurriedly backed the hearse up while getting ready to go and I backed right into a parked car.

It wasn't a bad crash. In fact, there was no damage to the man's vehicle. We got out of our respective vehicles and began to talk. The man was from India and I had a real hard time understanding him. I did understand one thing. This guy wanted money and was trying to say I damaged his car. He even went around to the back of his vehicle to look for damage. When I asked him why he was looking in the back when I backed into the front, he ignored me.

He then asked for my license information and business card and told me he would call me in the morning to let me know the damage when he could see better. I told him I wasn't going anywhere and that I'd call the police before I let him do that. He agreed, so we both waited. We waited some more, and waited some more, when finally I said, "This cop better get here soon or I'm going to be late dropping this body off". The Indian gentleman's eyes popped out of his head, and he asked me, "You got a body in there?" I said, "Yes", and he replied, "Okay we are not going to sweat it. I go now." Then he drove out of there like a bat out of hell.

The bottom line is that people don't have a clue when it comes to what we actually do during the course of our job in funeral service. They think we're either ghouls from the night or slick businessmen and women preying on people at their most vulnerable time. With everything I put up with in this profession, I have to remind myself that it was my choice.

LESSON 61—THE CHOICES WE MAKE DICTATE THE LIFE WE LEAD.

CHAPTER 9

Going For Your Dreams

Every kid has dreams. They may want to be a doctor, lawyer, or probably the most popular choice, President of the United States. What happens as we get older is that we lose our sense of wonder and begin to think a bit more realistically. Then we let our dreams go. It's sad really, because most of our dreams can come true if we cultivate them.

There was a commercial from a large financing company that made a lot of sense to me. It talked about dreams, and at the end of the commercial the announcer, standing with acres and acres of flowers in the background, said, "Let's face it, your dreams need more than just a little weekend gardening".

When I was faced with a medical discharge from the army, I had no idea how or where I would come up with the means to survive in the real world. The first thing I did was ask myself, "What do you want to do?" The answer was to be a funeral director. The next thing I did was to go to the library (Now you can go on-line). I researched every bit of information that I could find about the funeral profession.

LESSON 62—THE FIRST STEP IN CHOOSING A CAREER IS TO BE ARMED WITH EVERY BIT OF INFORMATION POSSIBLE PERTAINING TO THAT CAREER.

I became the proverbial sponge. I read books, magazines and every article I could find. I wrote to many colleges to get information on their funeral science program. I made phone calls and visited with every funeral director I could. I ate and slept funeral service until I knew all I needed to know. Not all the information was positive, but I knew exactly what I was getting into.

It was very scary for me to visit the colleges and inquire about what I needed in order to get accepted. All I knew was the army. I had three children at the time and no money to put towards school. I didn't even know how I was going to pay for more schooling. I asked myself how I would find a job, a place to live and a college all in the same area. Then I began to wonder about transportation. It seemed like there were so many obstacles that I should have found an easier route.

LESSON 63—OBSTACLES ARE THE THINGS WE SEE WHEN WE TAKE OUR EYES OFF THE GOAL WE ARE TRYING TO REACH.

I pushed, and pushed, and pushed, never taking my eye off the goal. The rest, as they say, is history.

Nothing comes easy in life. If you really want something bad enough, you go out and get it. It begins with a dream, but that dream must be broken down into goals. It's like climbing stairs. Each goal accomplished is one step closer to the top. There's a big difference between a dream and a goal. "I want to be a funeral director" was a dream. My first goal towards that dream was to gather all the information I could about it. Then I set the goal of finding the right school, a job and a place to live. My next goal after that was to get financial aid to help pay tuition. Once those were met, I began to set goals in the direction of my academics. I even broke that down to how many classes I could take a semester. Then with each class the goal was to pass with an A. Before I knew it, I was graduating and starting my career.

I've been blessed with accomplishing every goal I have set for myself so far. People ask me all the time how I have done all that I have. It's a combination of things, but it all starts with your attitude. The odds seem to always be against me, but I never pay attention to the odds.

LESSON 64—THE ODDS IN LIFE ARE WHAT WE MAKE THEM, NOT WHAT THE WORLD SAYS THEY ARE.

I didn't know the first thing about politics. Then somebody told me I should run for state representative. I worked on several campaigns holding signs at the polls and passing out flyers door to door, but that was the extent of it. As far as being a politician, there was no way. I thought of all the reasons in the world why it would be fruitless for me to even try. Then I thought of the one reason I should try because I wanted to.

The first thing I did was to go to the bookstore and buy books on how to set up and run a campaign. After reading them, I went to work. Having no money, I asked for donations by writing a letter to everyone I knew. Then I began to network with other republicans in my district. I visited the republican headquarters and solicited their help. They told me I needed to put out yard signs, and how to get them. I took some money from the campaign chest and had a few hundred signs made up. I recruited my kids and their friends to get the signs out. Again, I asked everyone I knew if they would be willing to put a sign in their yard. My sign ended up on republican's lawns, democrat's lawns, and any other lawn where someone had said yes.

LESSON 65—YOU NEVER KNOW UNTIL YOU ASK.

Before all was said and done, I found myself a New Hampshire State Representative.

Writing a book was another one of my crazy dreams. I thought I had a lot to offer in the way of sharing my experiences with some of the wonderful people I had the honor of taking care of. Again, I thought of all the reasons why I shouldn't even try. Not the least of which, I was not a writer. Then there was the task of editing and getting published. I thought about the hours and hours of writing it was going to take while working sixty hours a week and trying to bring up seven kids (more about the seven kids later). Again, the odds of ever getting published, even using a vanity press (which I did), were low. Screw the odds!

What do you think the first thing I did once I decided to write a book was? If you said go to the bookstore and buy lots of books on how to write and publish a book, you were right. Now you're catching on. I also spoke with a few local authors I looked up on line, and then I got started. After three years, I published my book, "The Greatest People I Never Knew," which can still be purchased on Amazon.com and other websites.

LESSON 66—TAKING THE FIRST STEP IS THE MOST DIFFICULT, BUT ALSO THE MOST IMPORTANT.

Did I make any money on this book? No I didn't. As a matter of fact, between the editor, publisher and the royalties I paid for the cover photo, it cost me more money than I had on hand. In fact, I took a line of credit on my home to do it. I had dreams of being on Oprah and maybe being reviewed by the New York Times, but it didn't work out that way. The point is, I dream big dreams and I'm not afraid to go after them. You do all you can to build a dream, then let the chips fall where they may. Joe Robie, the now deceased former owner of the Miami Dolphins, has an epitaph that reads:

LESSON 67—ALL MEN DREAM, BUT NOT EQUALLY.

At the age of forty-three, I decided I wanted to become a cage fighter. Now, think about this? Who in their right mind would think I could ever accomplish that goal? First of all, age does a lot to your body. I don't have the stamina I had when I was in my twenties. When I got injured, it took five times longer to heal. On top of that, I had three surgeries on my right knee and one on my left knee, which caused severe chondromalacia and arthritis. The orthopedic surgeon didn't even want me climbing stairs if I could avoid it. He also recommended I stand no longer than fifteen minutes at a time. In addition, I never boxed (unless you count in the kitchen with my father), and had no martial arts training.

Cage fighting, also referred to as mixed martial arts, is not for the faint of heart. Getting in a cage dressed only in fight shorts and grappling gloves (small gloves that cover your knuckles), to fight until you're knocked out, tap out, or are bleeding too much, isn't exactly everyone's ambition. Still, I wanted to do it.

Most men involved with mixed martial arts get out of the fighting game by the age of forty. There are some exceptions including former UFC World Champion, Randy Couture (another example of defying the odds). Here I was at forty-three just getting started. Now, I never expected to be anything like the guys in the UFC (Ultimate Fighting Championship), but that wasn't my dream. My dream was to have one professional fight.

While still working on that particular goal, I came close. The only thing that had stopped me up to that point had been injuries. I'd be set up for a fight, and I'd have to pull out from an injury caused during training. Perhaps the goal of a professional fight would not be reached for one reason or another, but that wasn't going to stop me from trying.

When I went to the gym to train, I got beat up badly. Jiu-Jitsu is great for getting in shape, but I didn't get through many training sessions without puking. The younger guys were stronger and had ten times the stamina I had, but I had heart. When training, I'd give everything I could for the entire four hours. Miletich Fighting Systems of Florida, where I trained, had sessions five days a week. If I wasn't getting my arms cracked from arm bars or being choked during jiu-jitsu, I was getting bloodied and bruised during stand-up. The sensible person would get out while still healthy, but who said I'm sensible? My point to this story is simply this:

LESSON 68—IF YOUR HEART IS IN IT, YOU CAN DO ANYTHING.

Never give up and never stop trying. Turn your dreams into goals and take it one goal at a time. Never let anyone tell you that you can't do something. Think things through methodically and be realistic, but don't talk yourself out of trying. Remember to set your sights high, but also remember that there are no shortcuts to success. Positive thinking is the most important aspect in reaching any goal, but it will take hard work, determination, perseverance and resiliency if you are to succeed. Don't let setbacks pull you down and always be true to yourself in every endeavor. You only have one life to live, so:

LESSON 69—DREAM BIG

CHAPTER 10

The Family

Every single person in my life has had an effect on me one way or another. Naturally, some had more of an effect than others, be they positive or negative. However, each member of my immediate family had something to contribute to the way I think.

I was sad to think that I didn't have a whole lot to say about some very close family members that I loved very much, but thinking back, there really isn't much to say. As far as I knew as a child growing up, my relationships were normal. Looking back, it was far from that.

My mom loved me as much as she could. She had so many other issues going on in her life that loving and nurturing me, or any of my siblings, was not within her capabilities.

One day she was down in the basement listening to her favorite music from Mexico, dancing and singing along to the music, when I came down to tell her she had a phone call. The music was so loud she couldn't hear the phone ringing. Apparently, she couldn't hear me coming either, and when I called her while I was standing behind her, she got startled and reacted by slapping me continuously for scaring her. Did I have some laughs with my mom? Yes, she was, and still is, a very bright, very funny lady when she wants to be, but all the other stuff overshadows that. She also thinks the world owes her, and she changes names and locations every couple of years. Her name went from Phoebe Ann Daniels to Diana Diaz De' Daniels to Fiona Siobhan O'Connor. Who knows what it will be next?

I still love my mom and would be there if she needed me, but I keep my distance.

My sister, Mo was the everyone's favorite. Mo was the nicest kid in the family. She still is, as far as I'm concerned. She never has a bad word to say about anyone and is always there if you need her. That's how she was as a kid and that's how she is today.

My brother, Ray (Sudsy), was a very personable young man and very intelligent. He had so much to offer the world that it is a shame he left us so soon in life. I felt so bad that he was always the hard luck kid. Sudsy left two young boys, ages six and four. It was a sad ending.

My brother, Anthony, was a favorite of mine growing up along with our baby sister, Dee. Anthony and Dee were so much younger than I was. I can remember pushing them in their carriages and changing their diapers. I was out of the house by the time they were ten and nine, respectively. I remember playing with them when they were young and teaching them how to pray and taking them out for ice cream. They were great kids who both ended up okay. Anthony is an Executive Director of a large Jewish temple in the Boston area, and Dee is a Quality Assurance Manager for a large jewelry distributor.

The other four family members I was close to while growing up were my grandparents. I was fortunate to have my mom's parents living next door to me my whole life as a child. If it weren't for Grampy and Grammy Kenney, God only knows where I would be today.

They loved every one of us kids as if we were their own. They never cussed at us, they never raised their voices at us, they never said no to us when we needed something. They took us to church on Sundays, to basketball games on Saturdays and to dance classes on Friday nights. They let us borrow their car, they opened up their wallets for us and they taught us the true meaning of unconditional love. All my happy memories as a child were with them.

My dad's parents lived in the next city over, so we would see them about twice a month. Nanny was a very loving and kind Italian woman with a heart of gold. Grampy Roy was more of a hard ass, but he would never hurt or deceive anybody. He had a tough upbringing. His father died when he was fourteen and he had to become the man of the house for his mom and younger sister. It showed in the way he would reason with himself as far as his frugality and stubbornness. They were married for sixty-six years before my nanny died. They were a Godsend I never really realized I needed, but looking back makes me thankful for what I had.

Family is important to me now that I have my own, but making the right decision isn't always easy. I'm sure my children could give you an earful about my mistakes. I wonder what they would write about me?

CHAPTER 11

Raising Seven Kids

Mary Anne and I were blessed with three beautiful children. Jessie, Stefanie and Joey were army brats until 1992 when our family broke up while I was in college. We got back together again after my graduation and relocated from Florida to New Hampshire. A year later, Mary Anne and I were divorced and I met Kelly.

Kelly was my second wife. She was the closest thing to a saint you will ever find on this earth. We married and I inherited two more beautiful kids, Ashley and Megan, who were eleven and nine at the time. Kelly and I raised them in New Hampshire and for a short while in Pennsylvania. Then I received a call from my divorce lawyer.

My lawyer informed me that my first wife Mary Anne, did not wish to have custody of Jessie, Stefanie and Joey anymore, and that she would pay me child support and give her rights up for the house in New Hampshire if I would assume full physical custody of the kids. I agreed, and Kelly, Ashley, Megan and I moved back to New Hampshire.

One year later, we discovered that my deceased brother's boys were wards of the state of Florida and needed a home. Kelly and I took them in as well. This is how we ended up with seven teenagers. I never could have imagined having such a large, diverse family in so short a time.

LESSON 70—YOU NEVER KNOW WHAT TOMORROW MAY BRING.

I don't believe that I ever could have done the impossible without Kelly. She showed them all what love, kindness, patience, forgiveness and selflessness was all about. She did everything for those kids. She worked sixty hours a week and still made sure that I was number one in her life. All that, and I let it go.

LESSON 71—APPRECIATE WHAT YOU HAVE BECAUSE NOTHING LASTS FOREVER.

Still, without Kelly, I would not have accomplished the things I did in the ten years I was fortunate enough to be her husband.

Bringing up seven kids from three different families was a challenge. My three were coming off a real nasty period where they were not very nice to their mother, and began challenging Kelly and me. Kelly's two were sheltered from the world, compared to my street-smart kids who were tough as nails. Then there were Matt and Josh, my two nephews, who were not only street-smart, but little punks from the hood. It was one challenge after another.

I made the biggest mistakes when it came to my first child, Jessie. I considered Jessie a friend because I felt bad for what she went through with the divorce, and I wanted to make it up to her. The problem is, when you treat your child as a friend, it backfires on you. Sooner or later, there will come a time when you must discipline your child, and if you treated them like a friend, it becomes almost impossible for the child to understand that you are actually helping them. They fight back like they are your equal, and you find you've lost control.

LESSON 72—YOUR CHILD IS NOT YOUR FRIEND. WHEN YOU LET THEM BE YOUR FRIEND, THEY ARE NO LONGER YOUR CHILD.

I take a share of the responsibility for all my children's mistakes, because they knew too much about adulthood without knowing the sacrifices and consequences of their actions. Today my oldest is the mother of two sweet children, Isabella and Giuseppe, and I can already see that she is not making the same mistakes I made when it comes to being friends with your kids. She may have learned the hard way, but she certainly has learned.

LESSON 73—IT'S NOT HOW YOU LEARN, AS LONG AS YOU LEARN.

Each of the seven kids had their own distinct personality. Ashley, for example was a hard worker, great student, very focused, tremendous athlete and purpose-driven. She was also very intelligent. Because of this, she always challenged our decisions and insisted on arguing with us. It's hard to win an argument with a kid who is smarter than you are. It's really the only problem I had with Ashley, because all in all, she was the most well-rounded and easiest kid to raise.

Her sister, Megan, was a sweetheart with a heart of gold. Megan was very good at school when she applied herself. You will never find a more loving and loyal kid than her. She would cry over anyone else in pain. She would give you everything she owned to help you. She would never turn away anybody at anytime, and she never ratted on her brothers or sisters, even if she got in trouble for keeping her mouth shut.

Stefanie and Megan ended up pretty good friends. There is a five-year difference in age, but the older they got, the better friends they became. Stefanie appears to be tough on the outside but is as soft as a marshmallow on the inside. She cares a great deal about others, and that's why I think she gets along with Megan so well.

Joey is exactly how I would want my son to be. We've been through a lot, but it was worth every minute of it to have a son like him. He has a learning disability for reading, and he has always struggled academically. He's extremely bright, however, which helped him graduate from high school. We always told our kids that we didn't care what they did when they grew up as long as they were good people. Joey epitomizes what a good person should be.

LESSON 74—IF YOUR CHILD GROWS UP TO BE A GOOD PERSON, THEN YOU DID YOUR JOB AS A PARENT.

My nephews, who we ended up raising through their most formative years, had it a bit harder.

After a few years of shuffling the kids around, the state of Florida finally decided the boys would be better off with family members in New Hampshire.

Kelly and I instantly said yes, but my father thought we had enough on our plate with the five we had and got us to reluctantly defer to my sister. Mo had two very well behaved daughters and a solid family life, so it was the best choice.

After a couple of months, it became clear that my nephews weren't taking to well to their new way of life and they finally ended up with us.

The first thing I did when they walked through the door was to hold out my hand and tell them to take all of their earrings off and give them to me. They both tried to fight it but I let them know that no male in my home would ever wear pierced earrings. I don't think there's necessarily anything wrong with other parents allowing their sons to get piercings, but I do think there's something wrong with my sons having them. Matt and Josh needed to learn what I learned years earlier with my mother-in-law. When you live under someone's roof, you live by his or her rules.

I always thought it was weird that our children were all so different. I was envious of the families that had two or three kids who were all "A" students. Not only were they "A" students, but also they were involved with sports, they volunteered in the community and were active in school clubs. I wanted all my kids to be just like that.

LESSON 75—SOMETIMES WHAT YOU WANT AND WHAT YOU GET ARE TWO DIFFERENT THINGS. WORK WITH WHAT YOU GET.

I had some "A" student kids in my family, but I also had truants, liars, fighters, learning disabled and attitude problems. I had teachers calling the house and cops at my doors. I had seasoned coaches who couldn't handle my kid on their team and other parents calling the house begging me to keep my kid away from theirs. Looking back, it really wasn't all that bad. In fact, it probably sounds a lot worse than it was, but it definitely wasn't the "Brady Bunch".

We all have our own minds and make our own choices. Still, kids are very impressionable, and a lot of what they do and how they react to things are learned behavior. Because of the way I grew up, I was never one to back down from a fight. That attitude carried over into my adulthood and was passed down to my kids. As a result, there have been way too many physical confrontations between my kids and other kids that could have been solved by simply walking away.

LESSON 76—WHEN CONFRONTED WITH PHYSICAL VIOLENCE, YOUR FIRST CHOICE SHOULD ALWAYS BE TO WALK AWAY.

I'm still learning that to this day. My attitude was that if you hit me twice, I'd hit you three times. If you pushed me, I'd push you twice as hard. If you had the balls to challenge me, I'd cut them off so you'd never challenge anyone ever again. A little attitude adjustment could have saved me many an ass-whipping. The same goes for my kids.

Jessie was particularly hardheaded and tough. She didn't feel as though she had to take anyone's shit, including mine. One day I got in her face and read her the riot act. She punched me in the face, knocking my glasses off. I wrestled her to the ground and held her down until she stopped. Did I provoke her? Yes. Did I deserve that kind of treatment from my daughter? No. But who taught her to be that way? I did. I can't really blame her because she had a good teacher. Jessie was, and still is, the funniest of all the kids. She laughs at all of my jokes and is the life of any party she attends.

Joey was a lot like Jessie in the sense that he had no patience for bullies. He would actually go out of his way to confront a bully. People who didn't know Joey would think he was a troublemaker. The truth is, the kid has a huge heart and would not stand for anyone taking advantage of the underdog. It was very difficult as a parent dealing with the situations Joey got himself into because it was always a struggle for me whether to discipline him or congratulate him. He was like Robin Hood.

When he was playing travel hockey, Kelly and I would go to rinks all over New England at all kinds of ungodly hours. Sometimes he'd have three games in one day. The first one was in our hometown of Concord, New Hampshire, at 6 AM. The second game was in Lyndonville, Vermont, at 1 PM, and the third one was in Massachusetts, at 8 PM. This went on for months and it was a huge sacrifice for us as parents to attend all these games when we had six other kids who needed our attention as well. I don't know how we did it, but we managed.

During a game in Salem, New Hampshire, our team was playing the travel team of Salem. It was a close game with playoff implications, so things were tense. All of a sudden, one of the Salem players crosschecked our youngest team member across the throat, and knocked him out. It was so bad that the medical staff took the injured kid off on a stretcher. Joey watched while they were working on the kid, as the perpetrator was laughing with his teammates at what he had just done. That rubbed Joey the wrong way, and I could tell when I saw him on the ice conspiring with one of his teammates that he was up to no good.

No sooner did the whistle blow for play to resume, when I looked up and saw Joey wrapped up in the corner with the kid who had caused the injury to Joey's teammate. The kid tried to crosscheck Joey across the throat. Joey instinctively started punching his adversary's head over and over again. The benches on both sides cleared and all hell broke loose. When it was all sorted out, Joey and a few others were kicked out of the game. While skating off, Joey told the other team to remember his number and that he would be waiting outside after the game.

I didn't want any problems, so I waited for Joey to come out of the locker room and planned on taking him to the car immediately. It seems Joey slipped past me with his hockey jersey on a hanger. He was outside in the parking lot holding his shirt up waiting for the other team to come out. By the time I got outside, he was squaring off with three other kids. I went out and broke it up before anyone was hurt.

As soon as I grabbed Joey to take him to the car, one of the kids from the other team said to Joey, "You gotta get your daddy to protect you?" It was all I could do to hold Joey back after he heard that. I told the kid if he opened his mouth again I was going to let Joey go. The kid mouthed off again. I let Joey go, and that was the end of that. Not the best parenting in the world, but I believe it taught the other kid a lesson. I was also prepared for Joey to get an ass-whipping, which would have taught him a lesson as well. This time Joey got away with it unscathed, but it wasn't always like that. He also got his share of beatings.

LESSON 77—IF YOU'RE GOING TO GIVE IT, YOU BETTER BE PREPARED TO TAKE IT.

There's always something going on with seven kids in the house. If one kid had a problem at school, the other had a problem with their boyfriend. If one kid was injured from playing sports, then the other was trying out for a team in a different sport. Anyone with a lot of kids will tell you that it's constantly solving one problem after another.

Ashley would play lacrosse in the backyard with all the boys in the neighborhood when she was in junior high. She decided she wanted to try out for a prestigious girls travel lacrosse team. She made the first two cuts and got selected for the team.

I was very excited and happy for her. Before bringing her to the first team practice, I went to the florist and bought her a bouquet of flowers to congratulate her. When we got to the practice, I told Ashley I had to bring Megan and Joey to the orthodontist, and that I would come back to pick her up. A couple of hours later, I arrived to pick her up and she was just sitting on the sidelines looking sad. She approached me when I pulled the car up and told me that the coach wanted to talk to me. I knew something was wrong.

The coach explained to me that there had been a mistake, and that another girl named Ashley was supposed to be picked, not my Ashley.

At this point, Ashley was in the car with her flowers looking like she just lost her best friend. I asked the coach to reconsider for two reasons. First, I felt it was their mistake and they were obligated to make it right, and most importantly, I knew Ashley was really good at lacrosse. I also said she would be a contributor to the team's success. The coach didn't budge.

As it turned out, the coach had a daughter who was also an excellent lacrosse player. She was trying to get her daughter into a private school in which "the other" Ashley's mother was the athletic director. Taking nothing away from the coach's daughter, I really couldn't have cared less about her education. Neither could my Ashley's summer league lacrosse coach. He ended up calling the president of the travel league and they made an exception to allow Ashley to play on the team. She became the most valuable player and led the team in both goals and assists.

LESSON 78—AFTER GIVING ALL YOU'VE GOT TOWARDS A GOAL, SIT BACK AND ALLOW FATE TO DO ITS THING.

Matt and Josh were the type of kids who made me proud one minute and upset the next. Handsome, well built and very athletic, they both were popular in school. Their talent lay in football. This wasn't Florida, however, it was New Hampshire. Certain academic standards had to be met in order to play on a school team.

Matt was a starter for a very good varsity team when he was just a freshman. In fact, the team went all the way to the state championship. The following year he got better and became a leader on the field, playing linebacker and fullback. Although he was doing well in football, he let his grades slip.

I warned him all year about the consequences of failing, as it related to football, hoping it would motivate him. I visited his teachers and his guidance counselor several times to keep abreast of his progress, or lack thereof. The school offered a tutor and the football coach even kept tabs on him with his teachers. After having a stellar football season and a very good lacrosse season as a goalie, he was happy and confident.

When the report cards came out, he had one too many F's to qualify for the football team his junior year. This was a crucial year for him if he wanted any chance to play college ball. This was a kid whose life goal was to play in the NFL. Matt figured the coach and everyone else would pull strings because he was valuable to the team and this was the year college scouts would be watching him. That never happened and he cried for days. I kept wondering where all the tears were coming from, because he was amply warned. The sad part of it was that the school provided the extra resources to help him succeed. Still, he couldn't understand why he wasn't going to be allowed to play his junior year. His choice not to study caused him a lot of heartache.

LESSON 79—THE CHOICES WE MAKE DICTATE THE LIFE WE LEAD.

Josh was a bit smarter than Matt. Seeing all of Matt's mistakes, he would criticize him. Josh would say what an idiot his brother was to blow the opportunity he had been given. If Matt was a great football player, then Josh was a superstar. He was the kicker, the linebacker, the tailback and the backup quarterback. The local paper did more than one article about him and he knew what he had and how to keep it, so I thought. Despite the fact that Josh's grades were inadequate, he got selected for a scholarship to a division—three college team. Many other teams looked at him, but after seeing his low academic marks, they passed on him. With two months left in his senior year of high school, he was warned that he was in danger of not graduating. He needed to pass a class he hated. Again, the school provided the resources. After talking all that trash about his brother, Josh ended up failing and never graduating.

LESSON 80—PEOPLE IN GLASS HOUSES SHOULDN'T THROW STONES.

Both of my nephews were given the opportunity of a lifetime. They were brought into a loving home with relatives, and they were blessed with athletic talent and a supportive family. For them, the sky was the limit. They didn't want to work for what they had. They expected things to be handed to them and that's just not the way life works.

Here they were, coming from the terrible situation they were in and doing so well assimilating into a well-grounded family, a beautiful city and a top-notch public education system. In the end, they seemed not to care, not to appreciate, and quite frankly, not to give a shit. Everyone in town who knew them felt bad because of where they came from. It was one excuse after another and they pointed the finger at everyone and everything except themselves. They were master manipulators and had a lot of people fooled into thinking it was someone else's fault. My question to them, even today, would be, "At what point do you take responsibility for your life?"

LESSON 81—IF YOU'RE EVER WONDERING WHO CAUSES THE MAJORITY OF YOUR PROBLEMS, LOOK IN THE MIRROR.

After raising all these children and doing what I thought was a pretty good job, I find as the years go by that I somehow failed. No matter how good I was to them, or how much I sacrificed, or how much fun we had over the years, the relationships are fractured.

My two nephews have nothing to do with me. They have gone on with their lives and I suppose they believe I was too hard on them.

My two stepdaughters, Ashley and Megan, chose not to speak with me ever since I moved to Florida and their mother and I got divorced. I like to think that I had a lot to do with their success, as they are college educated and doing well in life. All I did for them has been erased by an accusation that I moved to Florida because I had cheated on her. This time my reputation from my first marriage preceded me and it was an easy way for anyone to shift all responsibility to me. It so saddens me because the accusation is far from the truth, and whether anyone believes it or not, doesn't really matter. The damage is done and has broken a wonderful relationship I had with my stepdaughters. Our divorce was my mistake in a life's decision to move, thinking my wife would eventually join me. Once out of town, my past came back to haunt me and people were gossiping. If I were Ashley and Megan and were told what they were told, I wouldn't speak to me either.

LESSON 82—YOUR REPUTATION WILL ALWAYS PRECEDE YOU. BE PREPARED TO LIVE WITH THE REPUTATION YOU HAVE EARNED.

My three biological children, Jessie, Stefanie and Joey, are as stubborn as I am. Again, it all goes back to divorcing Mary Anne and the fact that I was unfaithful. There are so many unresolved issues and hurt feelings that it will probably take my lifetime, if ever, to resolve. Through the years my relationship with them has been a series of highs and lows. There never seems to be an even harmony between us. Naturally, in their eyes, it's my entire fault. Each of them has told me that I am better to other people than I am to them. I don't understand that, but it's the way they feel and it requires a lot of soul-searching on my part. In life when the loan finally comes due, you've got to pay up. I'll be paying a long time for some not-so-good choices I made years ago.

Bringing up so many children with such diverse backgrounds was draining. It was draining emotionally, physically, mentally and financially. We did our best with what we had, and made many mistakes along the way. Now that they are all adults, it's up to them to follow their own path. They are my legacy, and although I wish I could go back and change so many things I did or didn't do, I can only sit back and watch as they take on the world.

LESSON 83—YOU CAN'T JUMP ON A TRAIN THAT HAS ALREADY PASSED BY.

CHAPTER 12

Humor

Life certainly is not worth living if you can't laugh a little.

LESSON 84—IF YOU CAN HAVE ONE REAL GOOD LAUGH IN A DAY, THEN THAT DAY WILL NOT BE TOTALLY WASTED.

I've had a lot of laughs to go along with some of the trials in my life, and believe me; its what kept me going. Kids do some crazy things, and when you look back, you've got tears in your eyes from laughing so hard.

When my son Joey was 14, he and his friend Adam got in a bit of hot water with a female police officer. One night, Joey was sleeping over at Adam's house, which was two doors down. I got a visit from the officer at about 10 pm. I greeted her at the door and she asked me where Joey was. Surprised that she knew my son's first name, I told her he was over at Adam's house. She explained that the police had gotten a call about two kids putting a bicycle in the middle of a busy street, then hiding in the woods. Apparently when a car would come upon the bike, the driver would get out and move the bike out of the road. As soon as the driver drove away, the kids would come out from the woods and put the bike back in the middle of the road.

The officer and I walked over to Adam's house to ask them if they had anything to do with this situation. Adam's dad answered the door and told us he believed the boys had been indoors all night. When we asked them, they nodded. The officer explained that the bike was an old blue ten-speed. Adam's dad replied "We have an old blue ten-speed right over there", pointing to the driveway. We looked in the driveway and guess what? No bike. The officer explained that she had the bike in the trunk of her cruiser and offered to show it to Adam's dad to see if it was his.

While they were walking to the police cruiser, I stayed with the boys, looked them straight in the eye, and said, "You better tell me now if it was you or I'll kick both your asses right here". Scared shitless, they both admitted it was them, as if it weren't obvious anyway.

We walked to the officer and I let her know that it was them who did it, and that they had just admitted it to me. The cop got pissed! She shined the flashlight in their faces and gave them a big lecture on how she didn't have time to be chasing them in the woods when she had a city to protect. The boys eyes opened wide in fear as she continued to scold them.

Then she said something to them that blew me away. She said, "I especially don't appreciate running through the woods yelling, "Hello, hello", only to have you answer back, "Hello we're here", and when I got to the place you were at, you punks were somewhere else shouting, "Now we're over here".

It was all I could do to hold my laugh in at the sheer balls of these kids. I never would have talked back to a police officer, let alone screwed with them while they were chasing me through the woods. I told them it was disrespectful, and after the cop left, we all shared a good laugh. There's no way I could have punished Joey after that. It was just too funny!

Kids can make you feel so dumb. We had a raccoon getting into the trash, so I borrowed a Have-a-Heart trap from my boss so I could catch this thing and let it go without harming it. I put out a chicken breast for bait. That night, my kids heard rattling outside like something was in the cage. It was dark outside, and we are city people, so we approached the cage cautiously. I went first, followed by Jessie, Stefanie and Joey, one behind the other with our hands on the person's shoulders in front of them. It was exciting to us to be able to see a real raccoon we actually caught.

When I flashed the light into the cage, all we saw was a helpless kitten shivering in fear. My oldest daughter said, "It's a cat you dumbass!" So much for a city boy trying to catch a wild animal. I was informed later to put an apple and peanut butter in the trap. Apparently the cat would stay away, but the raccoon would still be interested. It worked like a charm. I released the raccoon in the woods a few miles away and we never had a problem again.

Just goofing around in the car brought many laughs to the kids and me. We would be driving along, and inevitably, came across some poor soul walking on a sidewalk. I'd beep the horn and when the person looked to wave, everyone in the car would be waving to no one on the other side of the street. Seeing the faces and reaction on those pedestrians was priceless, and the kids loved it.

Over the years, work has provided some laughs as well. I loved to vacuum, and make perfect lines on the carpet. After I vacuumed, I wouldn't allow anyone to walk on the carpet for fear they'd mess it up. Because I was so anal about it, the boys dubbed me "Captain Carpet".

One day a salesman came to the funeral home showing off the newest in household products. My boss asked the guy if he had a picture of a riding vacuum cleaner he thought I might be interested in. The salesman came out with a picture of some guy standing on this enormous riding vacuum cleaner. I should have known the company would never spend that kind of money on a vacuum cleaner for such a small place.

My coworkers put the picture to good use. They superimposed my face and head on the guy who was riding the vacuum cleaner. They hung the picture up in the office with big black letters at the bottom that read,

"Captain Carpet". I laughed when I saw it, but apparently they weren't done.

A few days later, I see another picture hung up in the office. This time, I'm vacuuming the sand in a desert with the Pyramids behind me. Above the Pyramids was the Pope on a balcony, looking down at me saying, "Does anybody mind telling me what the hell he thinks he's doing?"

I had a party in my backyard, which featured a pig roast and live entertainment. I was very excited because we had over two hundred people, tons of food, plenty of kegs of beer, and of course, live music.

I happen to favor Louis Armstrong, and I was looking for a band that played his kind of music. You see, the guests at this party ranged in age from three months to ninety-two years. I wanted something everyone could enjoy. I was happy to find four elderly gentlemen who called themselves "The Melody Men". The band featured a trumpet, a clarinet, an accordion and a drummer. I loved them! The party got started about an hour before the band arrived, and my buddies were well on their way to inebriated happiness. Then the band arrived.

These four old guys came hobbling into the backyard where I announced to my friends that the band was here. The leader asked if we could help them unload their equipment, whereby one of my friends looked at me, and asked, "How much can a bag of kazoos weigh?" to the amusement of the all of the other guys. Then my ninety-two year old friend just happened to be (barely) walking past us, when my other buddy says, "Is that the drummer?" I said, "Of course not, the drummer is in his seventies, you asshole!" The band started to play all the old tunes I love. After a while, the leader announces that the band will take ten. One of my buddies looks at the rest of us, and said, "Take twenty" another guy replies, "Take thirty" and a third says, "Fuck that, take a nap".

Then to top it all off, the accordion player had to stop playing because his fingers were hurting. As a result, the whole band got pissed at him and they all packed up and left. Consequently, the leader of the band was upset with the other guys and he returned his portion of the money

I paid, and quit the band. Now I have to live with the fact that it was my party that broke up the "Melody Men". I told you life wasn't fair.

We even use humor to get by in the funeral business. When my friends ask me if I'm going to cry at their funeral, I say, "Sure, for ten bucks extra."

Without laughter there is no life.

LESSON 85—LAUGHTER IS GOOD FOR YOUR BODY, YOUR SOUL, AND YOUR MIND, BUT MOST OF ALL, YOUR SPIRIT.

CHAPTER 13

Making A Difference

I know that anyone can make a difference in his or her own little world. Every Christmas I watch the movie, "It's a Wonderful Life", with Jimmy Stewart as George Bailey. It's a reminder how important each and every one of us is, and the difference we can actually make. The truth is, there's a little bit of George Bailey in all of us.

Making a difference doesn't always require great sacrifice. Sometimes a kind word or phone call can be the difference between living and dying. A few years ago I had what I thought was a nervous breakdown. During one of my episodes in my car on the side of the road, my daughter Jessie called. I answered the phone and Jessie asked me where I was. I told her, and promptly hung up. Fifteen minutes later, my first wife, Mary Anne, showed up to help me, which ended up saving my life.

My son Joey had a significant impact on some developmentally disabled classmates of his. He hung out with the popular crowd who had their own table in the school cafeteria. The special needs kids all sat at their own table as well. These weren't assigned seats by any means. It's just the way it was.

Joey decided to sit with two developmentally disabled girls who thought of Joey as their boyfriend. Before the week was ended, all the so-called "popular" kids were sitting with all the special needs kids.

That table became the popular one. It remained that way for the entire school year.

When Prom came around, some girls went alone. This one particular girl did not have long to live and was extremely shy. Joey saw her crying because she had no one to walk the red carpet with. When it came time for the girl to walk, she gathered her courage and meekly made her entrance. At that point, Joey who was in the crowd watching each couple walk the red carpet, jumped on the stage and escorted the girl down and back. Her shy, sad countenance turned into the biggest smile you ever saw.

LESSON 86—A SMALL ACT OF KINDNESS ON YOUR PART, COULD MEAN THE WORLD TO THE PERSON ON THE OTHER END.

Sometimes it takes courage to be kind. Junior high kids can be cruel, and everyone wants to fit in. One day on the school bus, Joey's buddy, Brad, was being picked on. Anyone who knew Brad absolutely adored the kid, so it was unusual to see kids being mean to him. The other kids on the bus kept their distance for fear of not fitting in, or of getting beaten up. Joey knew Brad was developmentally disabled and he wasn't going to stand by and watch a few bullies slapping and teasing his friend. So what did Joey do? He beat a couple of them up. Sure, Joey got suspended for fighting, but those kids never picked on Brad again.

LESSON 87—IT IS BETTER TO DO THE RIGHT THING IN THE MINORITY THAN THE WRONG THING IN THE MAJORITY.

Sometimes we do something seemingly insignificant only to find out it changed someone's life. While at one of Joey's hockey games, I was getting annoyed at the opposing goalie. The other team was wiping us out by a score of 8-0 after two periods. Every time they scored, their goalie would bang his stick against the post of his net over and over again. It was loud, obnoxious and was giving me a headache.

When the third period began, we scored right away. Three minutes later, we scored again. Thirty seconds after that, we scored again. This went on until our team tied the game at eight, causing overtime. I was so excited that I yelled at the goalie from the other team as I was banging on the metal guardrail. I remember looking right at him as I banged away. When he looked at me, I yelled "How do you like it?" It wasn't like me to say anything to any kid playing on the ice, but something got into me. He then raised up his stick and started yelling back, but I couldn't hear what he was saying behind his mask.

We ended up losing the game in double overtime by a score of 9-8, but it didn't end there. While I was waiting for Joey to shower and change, this young kid (whose name was Jeff Steer) approached me and asked if he could talk to me. I agreed, and he said, "I'm the goalie on the other team and I just wanted to apologize for my actions." I accepted his apology but explained to him that there was no need to apologize because I was the adult, and I should have known better. He accepted my apology, and said, "I just haven't been myself since my dad can't come to my games anymore". I asked him why his dad couldn't come, and he told me that his dad had cancer and didn't have much longer to live. This kid was fourteen years old. I felt like a jerk after he said that.

I thought to myself that his mom ought to know what a nice kid she had. I explained to her what transpired and I asked her about her husband. We talked for a few minutes and before we parted, I asked her for her address so I could write her husband a letter. She gave it to me and Joey and I headed home.

When I got home, I immediately sat at the dining room table and wrote the gentleman a letter. I described the incident to him and told him what a great kid he raised. I ended the letter by telling him he had no worries about his son becoming a man because he was a man already. I thought he needed to hear that from someone on the outside. I wanted him to die knowing he did his job when it came to raising his son.

About a year later, I came across a thank you note Jeff's parents sent to me a week after the incident. It said something about me being like an angel and that Jeff's dad really needed a pick-me-up after a bad week. I remember how nice I thought it was that they sent me a thank you, and I had saved it. Well, after coming across it a year later, I got to wonder how they were doing, so I called them.

Jeff's mom answered the phone, and I said, "Hi Jennifer, you probably don't remember me, but I met you at your son's hockey game. My name is Eric Daniels." She replied, "Oh my God, of course I remember you. We will never forget you". I was surprised when she said that, and I asked her how things were going. She explained that her husband had died shortly after I sent the letter and told me that some things happened in between the time I wrote the letter and the time he died.

Jeff was not doing well academically because of all of the stress with his dad. He had applied to a prep school earlier in the year and had just received a letter of rejection. Because Jeff was normally an A-B student, his dad decided to call the dean of admissions and explain why his grades were so low. He said, "I have a good boy here, and he deserves to go to your school." He then read the letter I sent to him and the dean asked him to fax it. The next day, Jeff was accepted into the school and eventually became the starting goalie on the hockey team. Jennifer told me that her husband was so proud and so happy for his son. Not too long after that, he died.

LESSON 88—IT'S IMPORTANT TO TAKE THE TIME TO ACT ON YOUR GOOD INTENTIONS. SIMPLY HAVING THEM IS NOT ENOUGH.

It always bothered me that my grandparents got old and lonely after we grew up. Because I was in the army, all they got was a phone call or a letter. I was only able to visit them when I took leave once a year. When they passed, I felt so guilty for not being there for them when they were always there for me.

Because of this, I make it a point to visit any elderly person I know who might be lonely. I befriended a beautiful little lady by the name of Betsy Manis. Betsy had lost her husband and I was the funeral director for his services. After the service, I told her I'd like to visit her and take her out for an ice cream. She said, "I might be eight-eight years old, but I don't do ice cream. I do beer". Now I visit her quite often with a twelve pack of her favorite beer. She out drinks me two beers to one and I truly enjoy her company.

LESSON 89—WHEN YOU DO SOMETHING NICE FOR SOMEONE, SOMETIMES YOU'RE THE ONE WHO GETS BLESSED.

Someday we're all going to get old. Between now and then, I'll make it a point to go out of my way to help others. Maybe others will do it for me when I'm old, and hopefully I'll be able to look back and see what a difference I made.

CHAPTER 14

When Dreams Don't Work Out

Here I am, at the tender age of 49, and people still ask me what I want to be when I grow up. It's not that I don't know what I want, it's wanting to do as much as I can before my time is up.

At the age of 16, I started out working in a leather factory in Peabody, Mass, where I grew up. My dream then was to become a salesman for the company making deals with shoe companies like Thom McCann and Kinney Shoe, who both had contracts with the family-owned business I worked for. I was idealistic and thought that if I worked hard enough in the factory, I could work my way up to a great paying job. When I asked the owner about the possibility of becoming a salesman, I was abruptly told that those positions were being saved for family members.

LESSON 90—IN A FAMILY RUN BUSINESS, BLOOD TRUMPS WISDOM, KNOWLEDGE AND HARDWORK EVERY TIME.

That became Dream #1 that didn't work out, and that's when I joined the army. The army, as mentioned earlier in this book, was a life changer for me. All the army had to offer and all the possibilities that lay in front of me at the time seemed endless. I took full advantage of the opportunities and did quite well. So well, in fact, that I set a dream of retiring as a Two-Star General, even though I was an enlisted man with no college education. After 10 years as an enlisted man, I found myself an E-7 (Sergeant First Class) with 2 years of college and was accepted into Officer Candidate School (OCS). I figured after twenty more years I would have reached my goal to be a Major General. It would have been admittedly unlikely, but still entirely possible. Before I got to OCS, an injury caused my medical discharge and effectively ended my military career and any dreams that came with it.

LESSON 91—FATE RUINS MANY A PLAN.

That became Dream #2 that didn't work out.

After the army, came mortuary school. Still idealistic and naïve, I was going to become the best funeral director in the country. I did well in mortuary school, and after graduation I planned on owning my own funeral home within a few years. The problem was, you needed money to start any such venture and I had neither a pot nor a window. After eighteen years of a successful career as far as making a living is concerned, I found myself no closer to ownership than I was eighteen years earlier. That became Dream #3 that didn't work out.

LESSON 92—TIMING IS EVERYTHING.

Then came the police academy. Getting accepted and doing well at the age of forty-eight was incredible. Police officer friends of mine told me that I would make a perfect cop. I was in great physical shape, I had military experience, I had life experience, I had an education and I had maturity that some of the younger candidates wouldn't have for years.

Halfway through the academy, I was given a conditional offer from the only police department that I applied to and was the only department I really wanted to work for. That particular police agency was one of the largest departments in the county and it was where I wanted to be. I was thankful to be selected by the agency, even though I had not finished the academy and had yet to take the state law enforcement exam. Being the old guy in my class, yet being the first in the class to get a job, was a great feeling. Everything was going perfectly.

To top it off, I ended up graduating with the top academic score in the class and was selected by my classmates as the most valuable player for making the biggest difference in their academy experience. I gave the graduation speech and my sister Dee sang the national anthem. I was on cloud nine. Everything was coming up roses and all of my hard work was paying off.

Then I started day one as a police officer trainee with the agency. I was very uncomfortable from the moment I stepped foot in the building. Being uncomfortable as I was, made me very nervous. It's okay to be nervous, but it's not okay to wear your feelings on your sleeve around the other officers who will be on the street with you. I found out quickly that any sympathy I thought I would get from my fellow officers was simply not there. I had this illusion that I would be helped with any weakness I had because I was honest with my feelings. It's best to keep your feelings of weakness to yourself. Cops have no time for what they perceive to be weakness.

LESSON 93—NO MATTER HOW STRONG OR HOW GOOD YOU ARE, THE SLIGHTEST SIGN OF WEAKNESS MAKES YOU WEAK IN THE EYES OF OTHERS.

The bottom line with the police agency was that this particular agency wasn't a good fit for me. I resigned after much thought. I realized I am better suited for a smaller department where I would not be lost in the shuffle of a couple hundred officers, and where I would have an opportunity to allow my individual talents to shine and make a difference. Even though I planned my course and every piece of the puzzle seemed to fit, it wasn't to be.

Am I discouraged? Yes. Am I hurt? Sure. Am I disappointed? Absolutely. Am I going to give it all up? Never!! Many people equated my stepping down and resigning from the agency with quitting. Quitting, to me, is when someone doesn't try and simply walks away. I tried very hard, over and over again, before I decided to seek other options and take another path. Sometimes we must concede defeat in order to be able to fight another day. Is it worth fighting a losing battle to prove a point? I don't think so.

LESSON 94—YOU MAY HAVE TO LOSE SOME BATTLES IN ORDER TO WIN THE WAR.

CHAPTER 15

Dealing With People

I'm not one to pull any punches. I tell it like it is because I believe in honesty, even if it's brutal. So let's face it, people suck! They are very difficult to deal with at times but it's not all bad. Learning how to deal with people in a positive and constructive manner is a life long process and you'll never run out of material to work with. Just as I say people suck, I also know that others may think the same about me. No one's perfect. One thing to keep in mind when sizing another person up is this:

LESSON 95—EVERYONE HAS A STORY.

My maternal grandfather was the sweetest man on the planet. Everyone who knew him, loved him. However, if you didn't know him and had witnessed his actions in public, you may think he was crazy and mean. Grampy didn't have an embarrassing bone in his body. Nothing embarrassed him, ever.

He opened up a bank account for each of his grandchildren at the local bank when we were little. Anytime I needed to cash a check, I'd go to that bank so I wouldn't have any hassles. The first time I went there I was in eleventh grade and needed to cash a check from a part time job. Grampy drove me to the bank and waited out front while I went inside. He assured me I wouldn't have a problem because he had accounts there for all of us. We aren't talking a lot of money here, maybe five hundred dollars in each account.

I got up to the teller and presented my one hundred and two dollar check. She asked if I had an account with them and I told her "Yes". I even explained that it may be under my grandfather's name as my trustee. The teller looked it up said she couldn't find anything, and, therefore, could not cash my check. I noticed two other tellers who I recognized from high school and three people behind me in line who I was acquainted with. Not wanting to make a scene, I politely told the teller I didn't understand why she couldn't find anything, but I would get my grandfather who was out in the car. I thought maybe he had a bankbook or something he could show them to prove I had an account there.

It was a hassle, but I didn't think it would be that big of a deal. So I told Grampy what the teller said and he exploded. He got out of the car and hobbled into the bank as fast as he could with his cane to help him. He cut everyone in line and went straight for the girl I was dealing with. He yelled at her, telling her he was going to take every penny out of the bank if they didn't cash my check. The teller looked again and found my account under my grandfather's name. After she explained that she had found it, he began raising his voice again, saying, "I should take all my money out of here you Goddamned bunch of yokels." I still don't know what a yokel is, but I did get my check cashed. If I didn't know the guy or circumstance, I would have thought, as I'm sure some people in the bank did, that he was a mean, grumpy old man. I'm not sure if the embarrassment I went through was worth it, but I do know he was standing up for his grandson and that's why he got so passionately upset.

One thing I have a really hard time with is people who just don't get it. Trying to rationalize anything with a person who just doesn't get it is like banging your head against the wall. You can't do it! The thing is, they're everywhere. Most of the time we see someone do or say something dumb, and we say to ourselves, "Does this guy even have a clue?" It doesn't really affect us that much, but every now and then we are directly confronted with someone like this.

Take, for example, a former co-worker of mine. He was a very nice man with a heart of gold, but sometimes I would be astonished at the things he said and did. He'd leave cabinet drawers open, not flush the toilet, and constantly use the wrong word for things. He would make up his own words to try to sound smart. Naturally, those made him look even dumber.

LESSON 96—IF YOU'RE NOT FAMILIAR WITH THE ENGLISH LANGUAGE, DON'T PRETEND THAT YOU ARE. IT'S EASIER TO LEARN IT THAN TO FAKE IT.

I had set up flowers in the repose room for a wake he was working on. I wanted to make sure I set things up the way he wanted so I asked him to check it out for me. Looking at one of the bouquets, I asked him if he wanted me to move it. He said it was fine the way it was, and that it was "invenerial" whether the bouquet was on the left or right of the casket. I said, "What do you mean by "invenerial"?" He said, "I mean it doesn't matter, its invenerial." I replied, "You mean "immaterial", don't you?" He replied, "I say invenerial".

I felt like slapping him and telling him that what he said was incorrect, but it wouldn't help. I've asked him several times to please close the file cabinet drawers when he is done looking through them. I asked him to please flush the toilet after using it, but asking him never helped. It took me a while to figure out how to deal with this, and one day I read Dr Phil's book, "Life Strategies" where he explains that some people just don't get it. Dr Phil goes on in his book to explain how to be a person who "gets it". It occurred to me that even I fail to "get it" at times, but for any of our lives to run smoother, you have to be a person who generally "get's it". Be patient with people and remember Dr Phil's words:

LESSON 97—SOME PEOPLE JUST DON'T GET IT.

Then there are the people who love to gossip. These people are particularly annoying because they make up their own version of things as they spread their rumors. I made the mistake of telling a co-worker and friend something I did that I didn't want anyone else to know. Not only did everyone find out, but also they were given false information almost costing me my job, to the point the Human

Resources Department queried me. Nothing ended up coming out of it because I never did anything wrong, but because of nosey gossipers, I went through a terrible ordeal. Again, I should have kept my mouth shut.

LESSON 98—MY FRIEND HAS A FRIEND, AND MY FRIEND'S FRIEND HAS A FRIEND. BE DISCREET.

What makes some people think they are better than others? Are they better because they have more money? Or is it that their daddy is a prominent person in the community? Or maybe they have three PhD's, and being intelligent puts them higher up the ladder than the rest of us? There's no good reason for anyone to ever think they are better than anyone else.

In my lifetime, there have been many examples of this type of person, but no greater one than that of the late Saddam Hussein, former Dictator of Iraq. He thought he was invincible, yet he was found cowering and scared, hiding in a peasant's hole. In the end, he was hanged for the whole world to see.

The other side to getting cocky when things are going your way and thinking that you are somehow better than everyone else, is that things change. Fortune is a fleeting thing. I saw that when General Manuel Noriega, former Dictator of Panama, had power, money and women at his beck and call. Now he sits in a federal prison waiting to die. It's simply not worth thinking that you are better than anyone else, because in the end, we are all equal.

LESSON 99—WE LAUGH, WE CRY, WE LIVE, AND WE DIE. THERE ARE NO EXCEPTIONS.

Dealing with angry people is always difficult. The reason for this is all the emotion involved. Somebody who's really angry is actually worse than somebody who's really drunk, because anger causes violence. I used to get so angry that I would throw things, break things and punch holes in walls. Every single time I got that angry and let the anger get the best of me, I ended up regretting it. It took years to control my anger, but it's something I had to constantly work at.

LESSON 100—NOTHING GOOD COMES OUT OF ANGER.

Then there are the cheap people. I hated it when we would go to a restaurant with another couple and they start adding up every little charge so the bill will be paid evenly. I understand not wanting to get screwed, but when you're with friends, you shouldn't have to worry about that. I started to pick up the entire tab whenever we went out with another couple. If I had to count my pennies that closely, I simply wouldn't go out.

I'm never stingy with the wait-staff either. These people work very hard and put up with a lot of unpleasant encounters from nasty people all the time. There was a waitress at a popular restaurant in Pennsylvania we would frequent. It was crowded one night and the service wasn't the best. She would come back to our table to check on us and just leave all of the dirty dishes on the table we had set aside for her to take. She didn't do any of the things a seasoned waitress would have done. We didn't get ketchup for the kids' burgers nor did she ask. There were a few other snafus, but I figured she was having a bad night. Everyone has a story, right?

My wife and I had a disagreement as to how much the tip should be. I thought at least fifteen percent. My wife was suggesting ten percent because the waitress did a sub-par job. I argued that perhaps it was her first night and management just threw her out on the floor because they were so busy. I also thought that maybe she's struggling with a recent death. As it turned out, I lost the argument, and she got ten percent. Before we drove away, I got out of the car, ran into the restaurant and put down more money. I gave the waitress the benefit of the doubt.

LESSON 101—ALWAYS TAKE THE HIGH ROAD. GO BEYOND EXPECTATIONS, AND YOU'LL NEVER LOSE IN THE END.

Not all people are a pain. At least some of us are just a pain every once in a while. I couldn't write about dealing with people by only mentioning the negative side to human nature. The nice things people do for one another give me faith that the world isn't all that bad. I always thought that it was the little things that meant the most.

I'm not a big birthday person. My attitude about birthdays has always been "It's just another day". Why celebrate the fact that you have one less year to live? That attitude is not the best I know, but I imagine it goes back to my childhood days when things were always bad. My kids and other relatives always respected my feelings and we never made a big deal out of my birthday. In fact, I insisted they not give me a card or even wish me a happy birthday. Looking back, I realize that I lost out on a lot of fun and that I denied other people the opportunity to give back to me, and that's not fair.

LESSON 102—DON'T DENY OTHER PEOPLE THE OPPORTUNITY TO GIVE TO YOU.

Just as I say I don't care about my birthday, I must admit I was upset when I didn't get my annual happy birthday song over the phone the year of my divorce from Kelly, from her mother and father, who have done it for the previous ten years. They thought it never meant anything to me because that was what I had portrayed. I thought it didn't mean anything either until I didn't get it anymore.

That year, I walked in to work at lunchtime and was surprised with a cake, candles, singing and a very funny card signed by all of the employees who worked for me. I was so surprised, and very, very happy. I never realized how wonderful it would feel when people did things like that for me. I felt like I was given a million dollars.

LESSON 103—DON'T MAKE A BIG DEAL OUT OF GIVING, BUT DO MAKE A BIG DEAL TO THE GIVER WHEN YOU RECEIVE.

Just as I appreciate all the little things people do for me, so do others appreciate the little things they receive. It doesn't take any money to be kind, too. Anybody with money can buy expensive gifts. Buying an expensive gift when you have the money at your disposal is easy. It's not as easy to clean the house, or paint a room, or give up free time to volunteer. When someone does something special for someone else, regardless of the magnitude, it doesn't go unnoticed.

LESSON 104—UNEXPECTED ACTS OF KINDNESS ARE MORE APPRECIATED THAN EXPECTED OBLIGATIONS.

I haven't quite figured out how to deal with mean people. It seems to me there are a lot of mean people in this world. What I don't understand is that the world is hard enough for all of us, without people being nasty to one another. Most of this nastiness is uncalled for.

I was watching my son's lacrosse game with a mother of one of the other players. We were standing close to the sidelines with everyone else, when a father from the opposing team, holding a video camera, stopped right in front of the woman I was with. He stopped directly in front of her and began video recording. She politely asked him to move over a step so she could see, and he told her to go to hell. Knowing that she was a widow, I stepped in and told the man to move on his own or I would do it for him. He mouthed off to me, but he did move. There was no good reason for this guy to do what he did. He just simply felt like being a jerk.

Some people are in a position of influence, or have a position that other peoples' jobs depend on, like the newspaper obituary person for example. They know that without them, an obituary would not get printed. So, funeral directors have to be very nice to the newspaper because if someone's obituary has mistakes or typos, it ruins the entire experience of celebrating a loved one's life. When that happens, it becomes the Funeral Director's problem, regardless of where the mistake was made.

Most people who work on the obituary section of a newspaper are kind, but not everybody can be like Laurel from the Florida Today paper in Brevard County. Every once in a while, I'll come across a mean person from an out-of-state newspaper. They know they can be as rude as they want, and get away with it, because I need them. One of the worst feelings in the world is having to put up with a mean person when they know they have you. All you can do is grit your teeth. The best way to get what you want out of a person like that is to kill them with kindness. Any other reaction is a losing proposition.

LESSON 105—THE BEST DEFENSE AGAINST MEANNESS IS KINDNESS.

The easiest way to get along in this world is to look for the best in everyone. I believe we spend too much time looking at the faults of others, rather than seeing the good in others. Also, if we put ourselves in the other guy's shoes, perhaps we will understand each other better, and we can all get along, as we should. Whatever we do is our own choice. And you know what I say about choices.

ABOUT THE AUTHOR

Eric Daniels lives in Melbourne, Florida with his wife, Denise. He can be contacted at ilwed@aol.com